Palgrave Studies in Compromise after Conflict

Series Editor
John D. Brewer, Queen's University Belfast, Belfast, UK

This series aims to bring together in one series scholars from around the world who are researching the dynamics of post-conflict transformation in societies emerging from communal conflict and collective violence. The series welcomes studies of particular transitional societies emerging from conflict, comparative work that is cross-national, and theoretical and conceptual contributions that focus on some of the key processes in post-conflict transformation. The series is purposely interdisciplinary and addresses the range of issues involved in compromise, reconciliation and societal healing. It focuses on interpersonal and institutional questions, and the connections between them.

Sandra Peake · Orla Lynch

The Disappeared

The Hidden Victims of Northern Ireland's Conflict

Sandra Peake
WAVE Trauma Centre
Belfast, UK

Orla Lynch
Department of Sociology
and Criminology
University College Cork
Cork, Ireland

ISSN 2946-2797 ISSN 2946-2800 (electronic)
Palgrave Studies in Compromise after Conflict
ISBN 978-3-031-64712-3 ISBN 978-3-031-64713-0 (eBook)
https://doi.org/10.1007/978-3-031-64713-0

Cover illustration: Brendan Murphy

This Palgrave Macmillan imprint is published by the registered company Springer Nature Switzerland AG
The registered company address is: Gewerbestrasse 11, 6330 Cham, Switzerland

If disposing of this product, please recycle the paper.

This book is dedicated to the families of the Disappeared, especially those who are no longer with us. Their courage, determination and quiet dignity in the face of the most unimaginable callousness and cruelty shine like a beacon in the darkness.

Series Editor's Preface

Compromise is a much used but little understood term. There is a sense in which it describes a set of feelings (the so-called 'spirit' of compromise) that involve reciprocity, representing the agreement to make mutual concessions towards each other from now on: no matter what we did to each other in the past, we will act towards each other in the future differently as set out in the agreement between us. The compromise settlement can be a spit and a handshake, much beloved in folklore, or a legally binding statute with hundreds of clauses.

As such, it is clear that compromise enters into conflict transformation at two distinct phases. The first is during the conflict resolution process itself, where compromise represents a willingness amongst parties to negotiate a peace agreement that represents a second-best preference in which they give up their first preference (victory) in order to cut a deal. A great deal of literature has been produced in Peace Studies and International Relations on the dynamics of the negotiation process and the institutional and governance structures necessary to consolidate the agreement afterwards. Just as important, however, is compromise in the second phase, when compromise is part of post-conflict reconstruction, in which protagonists come to learn to live together despite their former enmity and in face of the atrocities perpetrated during the conflict itself.

In the first phase, compromise describes reciprocal agreements between parties to the negotiations in order to make political concessions sufficient to end conflict, in the second phase, compromise involves victims and perpetrators developing ways of living together in which concessions are made as part of shared social life. The first is about compromises between political groups and the state in the process of statebuilding (or re-building) after the political upheavals of communal conflict, and the second is about compromises between individuals and communities in the process of social healing after the cultural trauma provoked by the conflict.

This Book Series primarily concerns itself with the second process, the often messy and difficult job of reconciliation, restoration and repair in social and cultural relations following communal conflict. Communal conflicts and civil wars tend to suffer from the narcissism of minor differences, to coin Freud's phrase, leaving little to be split halfway and compromise on, and thus are usually especially bitter. The Series therefore addresses itself to the meaning, manufacture and management of compromise in one of its most difficult settings. The Book Series is cross-national and cross-disciplinary, with attention paid to inter-personal reconciliation at the level of everyday life, as well as culturally between social groups, and the many sorts of institutional, inter-personal, psychological, sociological, anthropological and cultural factors that assist and inhibit societal healing in all post-conflict societies, historically and in the present. It focuses on what compromise means when people have to come to terms with past enmity and the memories of the conflict itself, and relate to former protagonists in ways that consolidate the wider political agreement.

This sort of focus has special resonance and significance for peace agreements are usually very fragile. Societies emerging out of conflict are subject to ongoing violence from spoiler groups who are reluctant to give up on first preferences, constant threats from the outbreak of renewed violence, institutional instability, weakened economies and a wealth of problems around transitional justice, memory, truth recovery and victimhood, amongst others. Not surprisingly therefore, reconciliation and healing in social and cultural relations is difficult to achieve, not least because inter-personal compromise between erstwhile enemies is difficult.

Lay discourse picks up on the ambivalent nature of compromise after conflict. It is talked about in common sense in one of two ways, in which compromise is either a virtue or a vice, taking its place among the angels or in Hades. One form of lay discourse likens concessions to former protagonists with the idea of restoration of broken relationships and societal and cultural reconciliation, in which there is a sense of becoming (or returning) to wholeness and completeness. The other form of lay discourse invokes ideas of appeasement, of being *compromised* by the concessions, which constitute a form of surrender and reproduce (or disguise) continued brokenness and division. People feel they continue to be beaten by the sticks which the concessions have allowed others to keep; with restoration, however, weapons are turned truly in ploughshares. Lay discourse suggests, therefore, that these are issues that the Palgrave Studies in Compromise after Conflict Series must begin to problematize, so that the process of societal healing is better understood and can be assisted and facilitated by public policy and intervention.

The latest book in the Series deals with an issue fundamental to interpersonal and societal healing, the return of bodies to complete the process of personal and social closure and to realise justice for a special set of victims. The Disappeared are a universal category, part of communal and political conflicts worldwide, mostly, however, killed, secretly buried and left unknown by states and their surrogates in conflicts with insurgent groups in order to disguise their breach of the principle of the rule of law. Whilst they became popularised in anti-authoritarian and colonial conflicts in South America, many conflicts before and since have seen enemies use this tactic to affront the rule of law. What is unusual about the case study in Peake and Lynch's book is that it was the insurgents who utilised the tactic; and not against their chief protagonists but against people within their own community. The Disappeared in the Northern Irish case are thus all Catholic and carry the accusation of dishonour, disloyalty and dissimulation that adds to the inter-generational trauma experienced by their relatives, and which gives an extra nuance to the families' feelings of injustice at their loved one's unlawful killing and secret burial.

This is a remarkable study by giving voice to the relatives of The Disappeared in 'the Troubles', and the vivid ethnographic material provides powerful testimony to their feelings of trauma, injustice and, indeed, anger at the calumny that The Disappeared were somehow justifiable targets. The Palgrave Studies in Compromise after Conflict Series has in the past given a similar voice to many of the key stakeholders in post-conflict healing, notably first-generation victims, ex-combatants, women, media, the religious, the displaced and civil society, and Peake and Lynch's book continues this rich vein by addressing a constituency that is 'hidden'. The Disappeared are hidden in a literal sense by lying in unknown and unquiet graves, but they are hidden in a general way by being unrecognised, unacknowledged and inconvenient victims.

Communal conflicts create many hidden victims, and this book is amongst the first to recognise The Disappeared and their loved ones as part of the reconciliation process in the North of Ireland who need to be granted more attention, time and respect. The number of The Disappeared in Northern Ireland, of course, pales in comparison with the tens of thousands missing in Sri Lanka, South America and elsewhere, but the injustice at their hiddenness is a striking stain on the peace process in Ireland as a whole, and discovery of their remains is important to personal and societal healing in the North and on the Island of Ireland. This is a political and institutional issue for the peace process, and, as Peake and Lynch argue so persuasively, also a deeply personal one for the families themselves. It should also be a concern for us all who live in an Irish culture where the dead—and their places of burial—are so ceremonially and personally honoured and respected.

This volume raises interesting and challenging questions about an important set of victims and their families. It admirably suits the purposes of the Series by encouraging us to recognise, acknowledge and respect those who can be neglected in a broad peace process but whose personal healing is part of a wider process of societal reconciliation and justice. This volume makes a valuable addition to the Series, and as Series Editor, I most warmly welcome it.

Belfast, UK   John D. Brewer
February 2024

PROLOGUE

I grew up in an idyllic rural area during Northern Ireland's recent conflict, often referred to colloquially as 'The Troubles'. Whilst I was aware of the violence, my exposure was limited. The Troubles did not affect us all and, whilst many were relatively untouched, in some areas the deaths were clotted thick.[i]

In 1987, at age 18, I moved to Belfast to train as a nurse at the Royal Victoria Hospital. There I saw the devastation of the Troubles first hand—the damage done to bodies and minds by bullets and bombs. The violence was evident in patients who lay on the operating table in theatre, in casualty, on the surgical wards, and in psychiatry, as those bereaved and injured struggled to cope and find meaning in what had happened. My sudden sensitisation to the Troubles wasn't just a feature of my day-to-day work, it was ever present when I was off duty. The nurses' quarters were situated adjacent to the Falls Road, and the contrast between my rural upbringing and my new life, in a conflict zone in west Belfast, was stark. The darkness that was peaceful in the countryside only served to intensify the feeling of fear in the city. There was an edge to living in Belfast that brought a watchfulness and a sense of unpredictability; anything could happen at any time; news of shootings and bombings travelled fast; the threat was ever present.

When I completed my training as a nurse, I worked in the surgical and theatre directorates. Given the scale and intensity of the violence during the Troubles, The Royal Victoria Hospital became world renowned as the leading accident and emergency hospital specialising in blast and bullet injuries. Pioneering and ground-breaking surgical techniques were developed, and lives were saved; but whilst physical scars were healed, the trauma largely went unrecognised. There was no mechanism outside of the family for people to share what had happened to them. The priority for everyone was survival.

In June 1995, I took a development post at a local charity called WAVE Trauma Centre. WAVE is a cross-community charity open to all people impacted by the Troubles regardless of their background. Working in WAVE I quickly became aware that the Troubles had left a deep and indelible legacy, and yet there was, and is, a blindness to the true devastation of the Troubles. Most violence was never publicised, but this was particularly the case for *in-group* victims, individuals harmed by a paramilitary group from their own community. The silence around these cases was deafening.

In 1995 a woman named Margaret McKinney came to visit WAVE. Her son Brian, whom they considered to be a vulnerable young adult, had been abducted by the Provisional Irish Republican Army (PIRA) in 1978; she believed that he was dead and had been secretly buried. When she approached the PIRA they denied any involvement in his disappearance and, in subsequent meetings she had with Sinn Fein, the leading political party linked to the PIRA, they too issued a firm denial that any enforced disappearances had ever taken place. After telling me her story, Margaret said, *'Love I don't know what you can do to help me'*.

In truth, I didn't know either. However, I started on a journey with Margaret and later with other families who also suspected that their loved ones had been abducted by paramilitaries before being killed and secretly buried. I have journeyed with these families for over two decades, supporting them in an advocacy capacity.

From the start, a central element of the work involved developing trust. This was hard won as over the years, many of the families had been threatened into silence and they lived in communities where the mantra was, 'whatever you say, say nothing'. Family members were naturally suspicious, and the fear was palpable. In some cases, families felt that they could only talk about what had happened when they were out of their own community and in a place where they felt safe. Whilst during this time there were periods when the PIRA and the Irish National Liberation Army (INLA) were on ceasefire, the violence continued, albeit at a reduced level, but the fear remained. There are subtleties and nuances with all conflicts and Northern Ireland is no different. There were unspoken and unwritten community *rules* and, in Northern Ireland, *not criticising the paramilitaries* was one of them. This meant that it was almost impossible for the families of those who were missing to highlight their loved ones' cases. Paramilitary control was ever present for the families and the threat of further violence was never far away. This was compounded by the fact that paramilitaries lived within the heart of their communities and the families were never sure who was actively involved in the violence, or sympathetic to it. In some cases, this even applied to individuals within their own families. The result was a blanket of silence.

The biggest breakthrough in my work with the families came in 1998 when I arranged for a group from WAVE to visit the United States of America. I wrote to the First Lady, Hillary Rodham Clinton, to ask if she would meet the group comprised of those bereaved and injured as a result of the Troubles. Margaret McKinney was one of the delegates. On May 7, 1998, we met with President Clinton and the First Lady. President Clinton listened to Margaret's story, and he pledged that he would do all that he could to get her son's body back. 10 months later, she and other families received a visit from republican representatives and they were told that a statement regarding disappearances would be released to the Press the next day. In that statement Oglaigh na hEireann (PIRA[1]) and, at a later date, the Irish Republican Socialist Party, admitted their involvement in the disappearance of a number of individuals.

As a result of this admission, in May 1999, legislation was enacted in both the House of Commons (UK) and in Dail Eireann (Ireland). This enabled the joint British-Irish Government-sponsored Independent Commission for the Location of Victims' Remains (ICLVR) to be established. The aim of the commission was, as the name suggests, to assist in the recovery of the bodies of those disappeared during the conflict. However, enshrined in the legislation was the guarantee that any information received by the ICLVR could be used only to identify the burial site and the identity of the individual disappeared. No other forensic examination could be undertaken of the site or the body; and information could not be passed to any other law enforcement unit or agency. Whilst the families may ultimately recover the remains of their loved ones, the

---

[1] Oglaigh Na Eireann is loosely translated from Gaelie (Irish) as Soldiers of Ireland. This label has been used by various Irish political and paramilitary groups since the 1920s.

legislation ensured that prosecutions and even the identification of any perpetrators would be almost impossible.

We know now that the list given by paramilitaries was not complete, and this caused huge disappointment to some families whose loved ones' names were excluded. The excluded cases remain unclaimed by republican paramilitaries to the present day. Despite this, the ICLVR included these cases and subsequently recovered a number of the bodies through planned searches; this included the cases of Charlie Armstrong, who disappeared in 1980, and Gerry Evans, who lived in the same village, and disappeared in 1979. Their inquests revealed that the pattern of burial in which their hands were tied behind their back and their bodies were weighed down with stones, bore resemblance to the recovery of other young men who had been secretly buried less than 300 metres away and whose cases were claimed by the PIRA.[ii] This led forensic expert Geoff Knupfer, to conclude that, whilst their deaths had not been claimed by PIRA, given the similarity with the other clandestine burials in the area, and the context and manner in which these deaths had taken place, they had been carried out by the same republican paramilitary group.[iii]

To date, the process with the ICLVR has been successful, but recoveries have been sporadic and not all of the bodies of the Disappeared have been returned to their families. I continue to work with the families to keep the issue to the fore. In 2005, following the visit of two family members of the Disappeared to the United States, a new search process was adopted using specialist forensic techniques. This led the ICLVR to adopt a new proactive approach, alongside existing investigative techniques; this has resulted in many more bodies being recovered. However, this process remains an information-led process, and the ICLVR continues to rely on individuals coming forward with information.

It has been an honour and a humbling experience to work with the families of the Disappeared over the last two decades. This opportunity to tell their stories is a privilege, and it is something that families are supportive of. My overriding concern in producing this book, and the study that informs it, was to ensure that nothing in the process would be detrimental to the established recovery processes, or would negatively impact the wellbeing of the families. However, the families are eager for the world to hear about their experiences and see this book as a way to have that happen.

Sadly, since I started this work, eight of the family members have passed away. It is comforting to their families to know that they told their stories and that their voices will continue to be heard through this work. Indeed, the families felt that through engaging in the study the families were no longer silent or silenced. Rather, their voices were heard and will live on in print. I am indebted to all those who contributed Fig. 1.

'Words mean more than what is set down on paper. It takes the human voice to infuse them with the shades of deeper meaning'[iv]

Fig. 1   Delegation from WAVE in the White House. Photograph @ The White House

In this picture, a delegation including Margaret McKinney (immediate left of the First Lady) meet President Bill Clinton and First Lady Hillary Rodham Clinton in the Oval Office, White House, Washington DC, May 7, 1998.

Sandra Peake
Co-author and CEO Wave
Trauma Centre

Notes

i. Smyth (1998)
ii. O'Halloran (2011)
iii. O'Halloran (2011)
iv. Angelou, M. (1984, pp. 106)

Disclaimer

This book is based on a larger academic project conducted for the degree of PhD at University College Cork Ireland. The data collected for this work represents the views and recollections of the interview participants. The analysis presented here is based on this participant data. The views of the participants represented here are their life experiences, as recalled by them individually. The book is not intended to be a factual timeline of events, but a presentation of the testimony of the families of the Disappeared. The publisher and the authors assume no responsibility for errors, inaccuracies, omissions or any other inconsistencies herein and hereby disclaim any liability to any party for any loss, damage or disruption caused by errors or omissions, whether such errors or omissions result from negligence, accident or any other cause.

CONTENTS

Abbreviations

BBC	British Broadcasting Corporation
CED	Convention for the Protection of all Persons from Enforced Disappearance
GARDA	An Garda Siochana
GFA	Good Friday Agreement
ICLVR	Independent Commission for the Location of Victims Remains
ICC	International Convention for the Protection of all Persons from Enforced Disappearances
IRA	Irish Republican Army
INLA	Irish Nationalist Liberation Army
IRSP	Irish Republican Socialist Party
ISB	Irish Statute Book
MP	Member of Parliament—United Kingdom
PIRA	Provisional Irish Republican Army known under IRA
RUC	Royal Ulster Constabulary
SF	Sinn Fein
UVF	Ulster Volunteer Force
WAVE	WAVE Trauma Centre

...   ...

LIST OF FIGURES

CHAPTER 1

Introduction

Abstract This chapter begins by chronicling the Disappeared families' journeys, in order to understand their experiences. By situating the experience of some of the Disappeared family members, it sets the scene for the remainder of the book. The chapter outlines the objectives of the volume and explains its focus on victims' voices and how this forms the basis for the chapters to come.

Keywords Disappeared · Family · History · Northern Ireland · Disappearance

> 'Where's your mama gone?
> Little baby, Don?
> (Little baby, Don?)
> Where's your mama gone?
> (Where's your mama gone?)
> Far, far away'.
> The lyrics of Chirpy, Chirpy, Cheep, Cheep sung by Middle of the Road, 1971.

When Middle of the Road released this song in 1971, Northern Ireland was already two years into a tumultuous period of political and sectarian

S. Peake and O. Lynch, *The Disappeared*, Palgrave Studies in Compromise after Conflict, https://doi.org/10.1007/978-3-031-64713-0_1

tension, involving violent confrontations between Catholic and Protestant communities, paramilitary groups, the Royal Ulster Constabulary (RUC—the predominantly Protestant local police force), and the British Army. It was against this background of violence that disappearances emerged as a tool in the conflict.

The first disappearance, that of Joe Lynskey, took place in August 1972. This was followed by the abductions of Kevin McKee and Seamus Wright in October 1972. In December 1972, a widowed mother of 10, Jean McConville, was abducted from Divis Flats in West Belfast. A further 12 disappearances were recorded over the following years, with 11 ultimately being attributed to the Provisional Irish Republican Army (PIRA) and one to the Irish National Liberation Army (INLA). One further disappearance took place in 2003 and was attributed to the Real IRA (RIRA), a splinter republican paramilitary group that rose to prominence after the signing of the Good Friday Agreement (Morrison, 2020).

Whilst many individuals simply vanished, in a small number of cases the victim's abduction was witnessed by their loved ones. The children of Jean McConville, for example, witnessed her kidnapping; they clung to their mother as PIRA members attempted to take her away, only letting her go when the captors promised they would bring her back; (Keefe, 2018) they never saw their mother again. In the days and weeks after the kidnapping, some of the neighbourhood women who resided in Divis Flats sang the words of the song *Chirpy Chirpy Cheep Cheep* to her children as they passed by.

'*Where's your mama gone? Far, far away*'.

The children were ultimately taken into state care. The same applied to the other families of those disappeared; they were ridiculed, ignored and abandoned by their communities, the church and the State. The fear and isolation surrounding the abduction and disappearance of individuals created a wall of silence that lasted for decades (Bew & Gillespie, 1999; Taylor, 1998).

The objective of this book is to give voice to those whose loved ones disappeared during the conflict in Northern Ireland. In chronicling the families' journeys, and understanding their experiences, the authors aim to conceptualise the loss experienced by first- and second-generation family members. Faced with the seemingly insurmountable challenge of pressurising paramilitary groups to return their loved ones' remains, the

Fig. 1.1 The shoes of Brian McKinney whose body, along with that of John McClory, was recovered from a double grave in Inniskeen, County Monaghan by the Garda Siochana in June 1999. Photograph © Cathal McNaughton

families of the Disappeared worked together to rehumanise their loved ones, to reclaim their identities and, in some cases, their bodies. Whilst there have been many remains recovered as a result of the families' determined and dignified perseverance, there are still more victims who languish in bogs or farmland across the island of Ireland. The work of reclaiming the Disappeared of Northern Ireland's conflict is not, as yet, complete. (Fig. 1.1).

This book focuses on one particular group of victims and their families. The loss of life during the Troubles was extensive and the perpetrators of the violence came from all parties to the conflict (Fay et al., 1998). It is primarily because multiple disappearances were carried out by one organisation (PIRA) as part of what is alleged to be a deliberate strategy, that the focus of this study is on the Disappeared and their families. This is not to single out or differentiate between those victimised by republican groups as opposed to those harmed by the State or loyalist groups; it is to examine how a specific strategy, a tool of war used around the world, impacted on those families left behind in the aftermath of disappearances in Northern Ireland. Furthermore, this work aims to highlight how there were a number of shared experiences for the families of the Disappeared in Northern Ireland, both locally and internationally. It also aims to demonstrate how the context of a loss has personal, family and political implications for communities; and to provide a greater understanding of community dynamics during conflict.

REFERENCES

Bew, P. & Gillespie, G. (1999). *Northern Ireland. A chronology of the troubles 1968–1999*. Gill & Macmillan.

Fay, M., Morrissey, M. & Smyth, M. (1998). *Mapping troubles related deaths in Northern Ireland 1969–1998*. Incore.

Keefe, P. (2018). *Say nothing. A true story of murder and memory in Northern Ireland*. Williams Collins.

Morrison, J. (2020). 'Reality check: The real IRA's tactical adaptation and restraint in the aftermath of the Omagh bombing. *Perspectives on Terrorism, 14*(6), 152–164.

Taylor, P. (1998). *Provos: The IRA & Sinn Fein*. Bloomsbury

CHAPTER 2

Setting the Scene: Disappearances during the Troubles

Abstract Whilst the violence in Ireland linked to Irish self-determination and opposition to British rule on the island date back centuries, its most recent manifestation, known as *The Troubles*, is generally considered to have begun in 1969 with a marked rise in political and sectarian tensions and a sudden explosion in inter-community violence. This chapter is not intended to present even a partial history of the Troubles as that would require multiple volumes. However, in order to fully appreciate the significance and impact of disappearances in Northern Ireland, some context needs to be provided to set the scene. A short analysis of *The Troubles* is presented here as it relates to disappearances in Northern Ireland.

Keywords Disappearance · Violence · Troubles · Sectarianism · Northern Ireland · History · Political Violence

Whilst the violence in Ireland linked to Irish self-determination and opposition to British rule on the island date back centuries, its most recent manifestation, known as *The Troubles*, is generally considered to have begun in 1969 with a marked rise in political and sectarian tensions and a sudden explosion in inter-community violence. *The Troubles* is generally used to refer to the period between 1969 and the signing of the Belfast Agreement/Good Friday Agreement in 1998 (McKittrick & McVea, 2012). The conflict is often over-simplified into two *sides*: Catholic (Nationalist/republican) and Protestant (Unionist/ loyalist); there were, however, many players within these categories, including the Royal Ulster Constabulary (RUC), the British Army, the British and Irish States, international supporters and observers; and, of course, the various paramilitary groups that aligned themselves with the main identities in the region (Protestant/Unionist/loyalist and Catholic/ Nationalist/republican/) (McKittrick et al., 1999).

This chapter is not intended to present even a partial history of the Troubles as that would require multiple volumes. In any case, count- less excellent texts already exist (Bew & Gillespie, 1999; Coogan, 1996; English, 2012; Maloney, 2011; McKittrick & McVea, 2012; O'Malley, 1997). However, in order to fully appreciate the significance and impact of disappearances in Northern Ireland, some context needs to be provided to set the scene for this book.

Prior to 1969, tension had been simmering for some time; the Catholic communities experienced widespread discrimination particularly around access to government housing and jobs, voting rights and the gerry- mandering of local/national election district boundaries (Coogan, 1996). Violence against Catholics by loyalist paramilitaries was an ongoing issue, with sectarian attacks reported as early as 1966, resulting in a number of deaths (McKittrick et al., 1999). In addition, mistreatment of the Catholic community by some members of the Royal Ulster Constab- ulary ensured that what was an already hostile environment continued to be so (O'Malley, 1997). In response to the mis-treatment, a series of civil rights marches were planned across the region and there was significant violence against the participants (Keefe, 2018). Further esca- lations in community tensions led, in August 1969, to the British Army bring brought into Northern Ireland in an effort to bolster the strug- gling police force. Initially, it was thought that the military might act as a buffer between Catholic and Protestant communities and, as a result, the troops were cautiously welcomed in Catholic areas. However, people very quickly realised that the soldiers were not going to be the protectors they had hoped for.

In July 1970, the army sealed off the nationalist Lower Falls area of Belfast and conducted house-to-house searches that resulted in the killing of four people and considerable damage to hundreds of houses. This became known as the Lower Falls curfew and was, perhaps, the final act in the poisoning of relations between the British Army and the Catholic/ Nationalist community in Belfast. By this stage, both communities in the area had adopted a siege mentality with vigilantes and nascent paramilitary groups assuming the role of community protectors (McKittrick & McVea, 2012).

During 1969–70 increasing numbers of people were killed by paramilitary groups, the police and the army. The result was that attitudes on both sides hardened, with cycles of revenge and hatred intensifying (English, 2012). In August 1971, 11 civilians were killed in the nationalist Ballymurphy estate by members of the Parachute Regiment of the British Army. On the 30th of January 1972, 13 civilians were shot dead by members of the same regiment at a Civil Rights march in Derry/ Londonderry and another man died later from his injuries (Bew & Gillespie, 1999). This violence had a profound impact on Catholic communities as it confirmed the belief that they were under attack and, importantly, that the State could not be trusted to protect them. It was during this period that the PIRA, a newly formed republican paramilitary group, rose to prominence within working-class Catholic communities (English, 2012).

As the violence spread, death, injury and the widespread intimidation of families followed (Fay et al., 1998). Nearly 2000 families fled their homes in 1972 as working-class communities became segregated along religious lines in response to the violence. Housing estates became defined as either Unionist/loyalist (Protestant) or Nationalist/republican (Catholic) (Keefe, 2018). Against this· backdrop, paramilitary violence, mass riots and widespread civil disobedience occurred. The manner of police and military responses to the disorder antagonised Catholic communities and, as a result, some Nationalist communities became 'no go' areas that the police and army could not, and would not, enter. In these communities, the police had lost what little credibility and respect they had (Dowler, 2013) and their exclusion left a vacuum and social control fell to the community itself; ultimately this role was taken up by the paramilitary groups. The British Army attempted to break down these 'no go' areas through Operation Motorman which involved the creation of substantial and intrusive military bases (Smith & Neumann, 2005); this further isolated the communities and hardened their positions, reinforcing the belief that paramilitary groups needed to take on a proactive *protective function*. The republican paramilitaries widely adopted the role of a quasi-police force in Catholic communities, announcing themselves to be defenders of their community from the police, loyalist groups and the occupying presence of the British Army (Smith & Neumann, 2005).

The discriminatory treatment of Catholics by various arms of the State was a very significant problem for Catholic communities at the time. Arbitrary detention and internment by either the police and/or the army was a common experience for Catholic men living in some areas of Northern Ireland (Norman, 2021). From 1971 until the process was repealed in 1975, almost 2000 people were interned in Northern Ireland, 95% of them Catholics (McKenna & Melaugh, 2023). Other highly significant events included the case of the Hooded Men[1]; a term used for the 14 men who were seized and detained by the British Army and subjected to *inhumane and degrading treatment* (Stevanovska, 2019). The men were subjected to white noise, sleep deprivation, stress positions and assault. Some of them were hooded and taken up in helicopters from which they were thrown out believing themselves to be high up in the air when, ultimately, they were only a few feet off the ground. As a result, Catholic communities felt under constant threat during this time and so, increasingly, republican paramilitaries were able to exercise control over the Catholic population. Ultimately, an informal criminal justice system emerged in the areas under paramilitary control (Knox, 2002; Silke, 1999).

It was against this background of increasing political and social control that the PIRA began a strategy of abducting, killing and secretly burying members of their own community. Disappearances continued throughout the 1970s and into the 1980s, with one single known incident taking place in 2003. In the same period, loyalist paramilitaries also carried out a number of disappearances, including the abductions of Hugh McVeigh and David Douglas. However, their bodies were recovered five months later because the location of their remains was provided to the RUC by one of those involved in the burial (McKittrick et al., 1999).

Although PIRA was widely accepted by their communities as being the only means of defence and retaliation, they did not have the unwavering support of their communities (English, 2012) and were often condemned for violence that was seen as excessive (Keefe, 2018). It is suggested that, following the disappearance of Patrick Anthony Duffy in 1973, a father

---

[1] A 1978 case brought to the European Court of Human Rights by the Irish Government led to a ruling that the men had been subjected to inhumane and degrading treatment but fell short of concluding that they had been tortured.

of seven from Derry, that members of the republican movement, some clergy and the local community created uproar by calling publicly for the return of his body (O'Donghaile, 2003). The recovery of Patrick Duffy's remains was believed to be achieved only due to public condemnation of PIRA by the Derry republican community (Elliott, 2014). A veteran republican, Mickey Donnelly, outlined the strength of opposition to disappearance at the time by stating that Derry republicans were *appalled* at any attempt to secretly bury someone (Breen, 2011). He added that every family had the right to bury their loved one with dignity, even if they had been an *informer*.

Despite the response to this disappearance in Derry, the PIRA and other republican paramilitaries went on to conduct many more disappearances during the conflict. However, it was not until the mid-1990s that it became apparent just how many individuals had been disappeared. Whilst it was long suspected of being a tool used by the paramilitaries, the victims' families were isolated and silenced and, as a result, were not aware of others who shared their plight.

A pivotal moment for the families of the Disappeared came in August 1994, just weeks before the PIRA ceasefire, when two mothers broke the silence surrounding the disappearance of their sons in May 1978. The mothers of Brian McKinney and John McClory spoke to a journalist from the Irish Times newspaper about the disappearance of their two young sons some 16 years previously (Breen, 1994). This was the first time that the story of disappearances had come to public prominence. Margaret McKinney and Mary McClory's bravery served to break down the wall of silence that had been erected and maintained around the issue of those individuals who became known as *the Disappeared*, in some cases for more than two decades.

A number of months later, Helen McKendry gave a heartrending radio interview to the BBC NI Talkback programme about the abduction of her widowed mother, Jean McConville, some 22 years previously (BBC NI Radio, 1994); she called for information regarding the whereabouts of her mother's remains. These two events dramatically increased awareness about the Disappeared in a community broadly oblivious to the existence of the practice. The families had lived for years with no knowledge of their loved ones' fates, of where they now were, or why they were taken. However, despite the publicity, the families' pleas were met with blanket denials of responsibility by republican leaders.

In 1995, Margaret McKinney wrote an open letter to the then President of Sinn Fein, Gerry Adams:

'I ask you Mr Adams, what do I and other heartbroken families have to do to have our loved ones returned? Beg? Yes, I will beg. I will get down on my knees or do anything at all that will enable me to put my son to rest. In the name of the Holy Lord and all humanity I beg and plead with you to bring our suffering to an end. Give me back Brian's remains'. (Original in private McKinney family archive).

It took a further three years before the PIRA gave any indication that disappearances had been carried out. In December 1998 they issued a statement calling for information on the Disappeared from anyone in the republican movement who had been involved in either the deaths and/or burials of those taken. Then, on March 28, 1999, some of the families were approached by representatives of the republican movement and told that the next day, the PIRA would issue a list of the names of nine individuals whom they had killed and secretly buried during the Troubles. It also acknowledged 'the incalculable pain and distress' caused by the disappearances (PIRA Statement, 1999). However, it is thought that the PIRA list was not complete and that the names of several individuals were omitted (WAVE Trauma Centre, 2012). Some of these cases have never been claimed by the PIRA. A further two disappearances were added to the list in 2009, and a further case in 2022. Some families suggest that the list of those disappeared is still not definitive and that there are other cases that have never been publicly highlighted (Oireachtas Committee, 2021).

International Engagement

The media and public awareness campaign undertaken by some of the families in the mid to late 1990s, whilst important in that it led to a recognition that republican paramilitaries had disappeared individuals, did not lead to the return of any of the victims' bodies. It took international involvement by the Government of the United States of America (USA) to move the issue forward.

On May 7, 1998, Margaret McKinney travelled to the USA with a delegation of bereaved victims organised by WAVE. Armed with newspaper cuttings and the only photographs she had of her son Brian, at that point missing for over 20 years, she achieved a commitment from President Clinton that he would have her son returned to her (WAVE Trauma Centre, 2012). Transcripts of the calls between President Clinton and the Prime Minister of the United Kingdom (UK), Tony Blair, the following day (May 8, 1998) reveal the impact of her visit (Staunton, 2016). President Clinton asked Tony Blair to work alongside the Irish Taoiseach (Prime Minister), Bertie Ahern, to establish a framework for a process that would enable the PIRA to provide protected information on the location of the bodies of the Disappeared. This would, in President Clinton's words, 'enable sanctified burials' (Staunton, 2016).

The involvement of the USA at that time was very significant for Irish republicans. Up until then, Sinn Fein officials had not been permitted to travel to the USA, but the recent granting of a visa to Sinn Fein Leader Gerry Adams was an extremely important public acknowledgement of the prioritisation of the ongoing Peace Process by the American Administration (Dixon, 2010).

There was, and is, a long-standing tradition amongst the Irish diaspora in the USA of using their influence on issues related to Northern Ireland. Gerry Adams, in his own book (Adams, 2003), referred to the process of harnessing US support for Sinn Fein's objectives in Ireland from various political and policy groups, such as the Congressional Committee on Ireland; the Irish American Unity Conference; the McBride Campaign Committees (focused on ending discrimination of jobs in NI); and the Ancient Order of Hibernians (Adams, 2003). However, the Clinton Administration offered the most significant engagement for Sinn Fein; not only providing access at a Presidential level but at a senior political level within the broader Irish American community (Spencer, 2019). In relation to the granting of a visa to travel to the USA at that time, Gerry Adams stated:

'The door into the United States had been opened. Irish American opinion was invigorated and informed. That potentially powerful community had a real sense of what was possible and there were new participants within corporate America, who were prepared to play a new role' (Adams, 2003; p156).

For Sinn Fein, achieving entry visas from President Clinton's Administration was critical; it provided access to huge fundraising (O'Clery, 2015) potential that could help Sinn Fein achieve its political ambitions (Smyth,

2020). Importantly, access to the US Administration also provided visibility and legitimacy, much to the chagrin of the British establishment. It was estimated that, between 1994–2001, at the very time the families were highlighting the issue of the Disappeared, 'Friends of Sinn Fein' collected over five million dollars, making the USA the largest source of funding for the party at that time (Maillot, 2005). The timing of access provided for Sinn Fein was also thought to be fortuitous for the families of the Disappeared; they firmly believed that Sinn Fein was encouraged via political pressure to *engage* in the process of recovery, and that there might have been limitations imposed upon their access and, by extension, their fundraising efforts in the USA if they had not (Staunton, 2016).

THE INDEPENDENT COMMISSION FOR THE LOCATION OF VICTIMS' REMAINS (ICLVR)

The timing of the campaign by the families of the Disappeared was *serendipitous;* had the families undertaken their advocacy at an earlier stage, it may well not have been as successful. The ongoing international dimension of the Peace Process negotiations allowed the families some leverage thanks to the personal involvement of President Clinton. This leverage was pivotal in encouraging the British and Irish Governments to establish an independent mechanism to facilitate the provision of information on the whereabouts of the bodies of the Disappeared. A month after the PIRA released the list of individuals they admitted to having disappeared, the British and Irish Governments moved to introduce legislation in their respective parliaments to enable those with information on the location of the bodies of the Disappeared to provide it, without fear of prosecution.

On April 27, 1999, the two Governments introduced legislation to move the process forward. The British Government passed '*The Northern Ireland (Location of Victims' Remains) Act 1999*' (The National Legislative Archives: Northern Ireland (Location of Victims' Remains) Act 1999, ,1999). This Act made provision for locating the remains of those killed by acts of unlawful violence before April 10, 1998, committed by or on behalf of proscribed organisations. At the same time, the Irish Government introduced '*The Criminal Justice (Location of Victims' Remains) Act 1999*' (Irish Statue Book, 1999). This combined legislation led to the creation, on May 24, 1999, of the ICLVR (also referred to as the

Commission). This legislation allowed the ICVLR to receive information that was to be treated as privileged; this meant that any information provided to the Commission could only be used for the purpose of establishing the location and the identity of the victims' remains, and not for any other investigative purpose such as the forensic analysis of any weapons used or the analysis of any other material.

Four days after the legislation passed into law in both Parliaments, the Irish police force, An Garda Siochana (AGS)[2] and a priest received calls telling them that the body of Eamon Molloy could be found in a coffin, in a graveyard in Faughart, County Louth. It was thought that the body had been exhumed from a clandestine burial site located somewhere else, and then placed in a new coffin before being brought to Faughart Cemetery in the Republic of Ireland (BBC News, 1999a). It was a case that had previously been unknown. As Eamon's brother Michael states,

> 'It wasn't until 1999 that we finally found out what happened to him. A woman my mother knew from Sinn Fein got in touch to say there had been a development with regard to The Disappeared. This was the first time we had ever heard of The Disappeared so we were somewhat surprised to hear this news. The woman said that Eamon's name was on a list of people taken away by the IRA and executed and that we would shortly be getting his remains back. It came as quite a shock to us all but especially my mother as she never thought that he was dead' (WAVE, 2012).

Other burial sites were identified across Ireland and the Gardai undertook a series of searches. Initially, these searches failed to recover any of the victims' remains. Media interviews with the families at the time indicate that buoyed by the early recovery of Eamon Molloy's body, they all expected recovery of their loved ones within days (BBC NI News, 1999b). In June 1999, on the eve of the searches being adjourned, the Gardai located the shoes of Brian McKinney and John McClory ultimately leading to their recovery from a grave in Inniskeen, again in the border county of Louth. Following a further unsuccessful period of searching, the searches for the rest of the Disappeared were then ended.

In August 2003, a man out walking with his grandchildren on Shelling Hill beach in County Louth came across clothing and bone embedded within the sand. A subsequent search by the Gardai identified the remains

---

[2] AGS are also often referred to as The Gardai/Guards,

as those of Jean McConville (Keefe, 2018). An extensive search for Jean had been undertaken in the neighbouring beach at Templeton, County Louth during 1999/2000, to no avail. The *accidental* way Jean's body was recovered meant that the protections afforded by the ICLVR legislation against prosecution did not apply. However, although all the usual criminal justice options (e.g. forensic analysis) were available to the authorities, this case was treated in line with the ICLVR legislative framework.[3]

Emboldened by the recovery of these remains, the families continued to highlight their loved ones' cases. A further two visits were undertaken to the USA. Following one of the visits, in May 2004, and after a meeting with Mitchell Reiss, the US Envoy to Northern Ireland, Anna McShane (the daughter of Charlie Armstrong, disappeared in August 1980) and Anne Morgan (the sister of Seamus Ruddy, disappeared in May 1985) returned and lobbied for a forensic approach to be adopted in the search process (WAVE, 2012). The family members sought the use of ground penetrating radar and other forensic techniques, rather than a reliance on the recollections of individuals who came forward with information. The families lobbied the ICLVR and other Government ministers leading to the appointment of Geoff Knupfer, a forensic scientist and former Detective Chief Inspector with the Greater Manchester Police. Geoff had previously worked to recover the bodies of the children killed and secretly buried by the 'Moors Murderers', Ian Brady and Myra Hindley (Brophy, 2017). The adoption of a forensic approach, in terms of how information was gathered and analysed and the deployment of specialist contractors and a dedicated team of forensic archaeologists, was a significant step forward in the quest to recover the bodies of those disappeared as up until this point, the searches were carried out by the police. However, the ICLVR continued to rely on an information-led approach and did and still do not carry out speculative searches.

At the time of writing, fourteen bodies have been recovered. The first known recovery was that of Eugene Simons, in 1984, prior to the establishment of the ICLVR. Eugene's body was found following the draining of a bog in County Louth; he was disappeared on New Year's Day 1981. The body of Eamon Molloy was located in a graveyard in Faughart, County Louth, in May 1999 (immediately after the ICLVR legislation

---

[3] See the Inquest into the death of Jean Mc Conville (Dundalk Coroners Court, April 6, 2004).

came into law). This was followed by An Garda Siochana's recovery of the bodies of Brian McKinney and John McClory in June 1999; Jean McConville' remains were recovered in 2003. Since then, eight bodies have been recovered by the ICLVR forensic team: Danny McIlhone in 2008; Charlie Armstrong, Gerry Evans and Peter Wilson in 2010; Brendan Megraw in 2014; Kevin McKee and Seamus Wright in 2015 and Seamus Ruddy in 2017. Gareth O'Connor was abducted in 2003 by the Real IRA (a splinter group that emerged from the PIRA) WAVE Trauma Centre (2012) — his body was recovered in his submerged car in Victoria Quay, in Omeath, County Louth in 2005. However, this case falls outside the remit of the ICLVR which covers disappearances perpetrated *prior to* the 1998 Good Friday Agreement (ICLVR, 2020).

THE STRATEGY OF DISAPPEARANCE

For years there has been speculation amongst the families as to whether or not disappearances were sanctioned by the leaders of the republican paramilitary groups. For example, the documentary 'I Dolours', (IMDbPro, 2018) which focused on the life of Dolours Price, a PIRA volunteer, states that the abductions carried out by the PIRA were sanctioned by a specific *group* within the PIRA, and undertaken by a faction referred to as the 'Unknowns' (Maloney, 2011). This assertion has always been denied by republican leadership (McDonald, 2018). However, based on accounts that detail the activities of these 'Unknowns', disappearances were not ad hoc, rather, it is suggested that they were part of a specific strategy adopted by a number of republican paramilitary active service units (Maloney, 2011).

The research study which informs this book focuses on this particular group of victims and their families. This is primarily because multiple disappearances were carried out by one organisation (PIRA) as part of what is assumed to be a deliberate strategy (i.e. to ensure that all traces of the Disappeared victims' existence were obliterated, and that control was maintained over their families and the community). Access to the families of those disappeared in this way allows the researchers to understand how patterns in the disappearances and their aftermath impacted the families and to explore the implications. The book aims to demonstrate how the act of disappearance has a profound and very specific transgenerational impact. Furthermore, it seeks to highlight how there are many shared experiences for the families of the Disappeared, and to compare those to local cases, as well as disappearances carried out internationally.

REFERENCES

Adams, G. (2003). *A farther shore. Ireland's long road to peace*. Random House.

BBC News. (1999a). Disappeared return to haunt Ireland's conscience. *BBC Online Network*. June 7, 1999. Available online at https://news.bbc.co.uk/1/hi/programmes/from_our_own_correspondent/362314.stm (Accessed: January 12 2020).

BBC News. (1999b). Tragedies of the troubles. *BBC News Online Network*. May 28. Available at: https://news.bbc.co.uk/1/hi/uk/355240.stm (Accessed: December 30 2021).

BBC NI Radio. (1994). Best of Talk Back Programme (incl December 7 1994): Radio interview with David Dunseith. *BBC NI Radio Ulster*. December 10 1994. Retrieved from the Listening and Viewing Service, Rare Books and Music Reading Room, Boston Spa Yorkshire.

Bew, P. & Gillespie, G. (1999). *Northern Ireland. A chronology of the troubles. 1968–1999*. Gill & Macmillan.

Breen, S. (1994). Missing presumed dead. *The Irish Times*, 13 August. Available at: https://www.irishtimes.com/newspaper/archive/1994/0813/Pg027.htm#Ar02700 (Accessed: August 12 2021).

Breen, S. (2011). McGuinness unit told to stop having informers disappear. *Irish Mail on Sunday*, 2 October. Available at: https://www.nzhound.com/articles/breen/arts2011/oct2_Stop_having_informers_disappeared_SBreen_Irish-Mail-on-Sunday.php (Accessed: December 12 2021).

Brophy, D. (2017). As long as there is work to do we'll continue it: The lead detective searching for the remains of the disappeared. *The Journal*, 29 December. Available at: https://www.thejournal.ie/geoff-knupfer-the-disappeared-interview-375810-Dec2017/ (Accessed: September 12 2021).

Coogan, T. (1996). *The troubles. Ireland's ordeal 1966–1196 and the search for peace*. Arrow Publishing.

Dixon, P. (2010). Rosy catholics, Dour prods: President clinton and the Northern Ireland peace process. *International Politics*, 47(2), 210–228.

Dowler, L. (2013). Waging hospitality: Feminist geopolitics and tourism in West Belfast Northern Ireland. *Geopolitics*, 18(4), 779–799

Elliott, T. (2014). *Did Martin McGuinness pull the wool over marion finucane's eyes?' The broken elbow*. An online blog. Available at: https://thebrokenelbow.com/2014/06/10/did-martin-mcguiness-pull-the-wool-over-marian-finucane-eyes/ (Accessed: December 12 2021)

English, R. (2012). *Armed struggle. The history of the IRA*. Pan Books.

Fay, M., Morrissey, M. & Smyth, M. (1998). *Mapping troubles related deaths in Northern Ireland 1969–1998*. Incore.

ICLVR. (2020). *Introduction to ICLVR, An coimisiun neamhspleach um aimsiu taisi iospartach. Independent Commission for the location of victims remains*. Available at: http://iclvr.ie/ (Accessed: March 16 2020).

IMDbPro. (2018). *I, Dolours. One women's story of life and death in the IRA*. 31 August. Available at: https://imdb.com/title/tt8649148/ (Accessed: December 12 2021).

IRA Statement. (1999). Irish republican army statement on the disappeared march 30 1999. In Rowan, B. (Ed.) (2015) *Unfinished peace. Thoughts on Northern Ireland's unanswered past*. Colourprint.

Irish Statue Book. (1999). Criminal justice (Location of victims' remains) Act 1999. Number 9 of 1999. *Irish Statute Book (ISB)*. Available at: https://www.irishstatutebook.ie/eli/1999/act/9/enacted/en/print.html (Accessed: October 12 2021).

Keefe, P. (2018). *Say nothing. A true story of murder and memory in Northern Ireland*. Williams Collins.

Knox, C. (2002). See no evil, Hear no evil. *British Journal of Criminology, 42*(1), 164–185.

Maillot, A. (2005). *New sinn fein. Irish republicanism in the twenty-first century*. Routledge.

Maloney, E. (2011). *Voices from the grave*. Faber & Faber.

McDonald, H. (2018). British Army knew of IRA unit before it took the disappeared. *The Guardian*, 1 April. Available at: https://www.theguardian.com/uk-news/2-18/apr/01/british-army-knew-of-ira-unit-before-it-took-the-disappeared (Accessed: January 12 2022).

McKenna, F. & Melaugh, M. (2023). *Key events - internment (1971–1975) cain archive*. Available at: https://cain.ulster.ac.uk/events/intern/index.html (Accessed: January 5 2024).

McKittrick, D. & McVea, D. (2012). *Making sense of the troubles*. Penguin Viking.

McKittrick, D., Kelters, S., Feeney, B. & Thornton, C. (1999). Lost lives. *The stories of the men, Women and children who died as a result of the Northern Ireland Troubles*. Mainstream Publishing.

Norman, J. (2021). Negotiating detention: The radical pragmatism of prison – based resistance in protracted conflicts. *Security Dialogue*, January, pp. 1–17. Available at: https://https://doi.org/10.1177/096701 062097-521 (Accessed: November 10 2021).

Northern Ireland (Location of Victims' Remains) Act 1999. (1999). *The national legislative archives*. Available at: https://www.legislation.gov.uk/ukpga/1999/7/contents (Accessed: October 12 2021).

O'Clery, C. (2015). *How supporting Sinn Fein became respectable for Irish Americans*, The Irish Times 6 March. Available at: https://www.irishtimes.com/new/politics/how-supporting-sinn-fein-became-respectable-for-irish-americans-1.2129205 (Accessed: January 6 2024).

O'Donghaile, D. (2003). *Derry's Disappeared, The Blanket: A Journal of Protest and Dissent*. Available at: https://indiamond6.ulib.iupui.edu:81/derrysdisappeared.html (Accessed: December 2 2021).

O'Malley, P. (1997). *The uncivil wars*. Beacon Press.

Oireachtas. (2021). Good friday committee to discuss the issue of the disappeared with representatives from the WAVE trauma centre. *The Joint Committee on the Implementation of the Good Friday Agreement*. 9 December. Available at: https://data.oireactas.ie/ie/oireactas/debateRecord/joint_committe_on_the_good_friday_agreement/2021-12-09/debate/mul@/main.pdf (Accessed: December 12 2021).

Silke, A. (1999). Rebel's dilemma: The changing relationship between the IRA, Sinn Fein and paramilitary vigilantism in Northern Ireland. *Terrorism and Political Violence, 11*(1), 55–93.

Smith, M., & Neumann, P. (2005). Motorman's long journey: Changing the strategic setting in Northern Ireland. *Contemporary British History, 19*(4), 413–435.

Smyth, T. (2020). Irish American organisations and the Northern Ireland conflict in the 1980's: Heightened political agency and ethnic vitality. *Journal of American Ethnic History, 39*(2), 36–61.

Spencer, G. (2019). Motivation and intervention in the Northern Ireland peace process: An interview with president clinton. *Negotiation Journal, 35*(2), 269–296.

Staunton, D. (2016). *Troubles never far from topic of Blair and Clinton talks*, irishtimes.com, 8 January. Available at: https://www.irishtimes.com/news/politics/troubles-never-far-from-topic-of-blair-and-clinton-talks-1.2490245 (Accessed: June 13 2020).

Stevanovska, V. (2019). *Reassessment of the Ireland v. the United Kingdom ECtHR case: A lost opportunity to clarify the Distinction between Torture and Ill-Treatment: Torture Journal, 29* (1), 56–69

WAVE. (2012). The story of Brian McKinney. In WAVE (Ed.) *The disappeared of Northern Ireland's troubles*. WAVE Trauma Centre.

CHAPTER 3

Historical Disappearances and International Cases

Abstract In Ireland, the practice of abducting, murdering and secretly burying individuals did not begin during the Troubles. Throughout the Independence Conflict period, which included both the War of Independence (1919–1921), and the Irish Civil War (1922–1923), the abduction, murder and disappearance of individuals was a common occurrence carried out by paramilitaries and State forces alike. Only recently, however, have the disappearances that took place during this period of history garnered greater prominence in academic study and historical accounts. The disappearances of the Independence Conflict period, and the outcomes for the families and communities involved, is relevant to the study of the disappearances that took place during the Troubles for a number of reasons, not least of these is the direct impact the practice had on the families of those who were left behind. This chapter explores historic disappearances and their relevance from the Troubles, whilst also exploring the international context of disappearances more generally.

Keywords Disappearance · Irish Civil War · War of Independence · History · International Disappearances

S. Peake and O. Lynch, *The Disappeared*, Palgrave Studies in Compromise after Conflict,
https://doi.org/10.1007/978-3-031-64713-0_3

In Ireland, the practice of abducting, murdering and secretly burying individuals did not begin during the Troubles. Throughout the Independence Conflict period, that included both the War of Independence (1919–1921), and the Irish Civil War (1922–1923), the abduction, murder and disappearance of individuals was a common occurrence carried out by paramilitaries and State forces alike. Only recently, however, have the disappearances that took place during this period of history garnered greater prominence in academic study and historical accounts (Borgonova, 2007; Hart, 2009; Murphy, 2011; Fitzpatrick, 2013; O'Halpin, 2013; Bielenberg & Donnelly, 2016; O'Ruairc, 2016; Bielenberg & O'Ruairc, 2020a).

The disappearances of the Independence Conflict period, and the outcomes for the families and communities involved, is relevant to the study of the disappearances that took place during the Troubles for a number of reasons, not least of these is the direct impact the practice had on the families of those who were left behind. Using a range of strategies, the paramilitaries at that time enforced a silence around the disappearances that ensured that the families were marginalised and that the community and wider society were similarly quieted; this silence lasted decades.

In assessing the relevance of historic disappearances, it is important to first consider the context in which they occurred. The Irish War of Independence was fought by the Irish Republican Army (IRA) against the British security forces. It ended with a ceasefire on July 11, 1921, and the signing of the subsequent Anglo-Irish Treaty on December 6, 1921. This treaty resulted in the creation of a border on the island of Ireland, with the Irish Free State comprising 26 counties and six counties of Ulster making up Northern Ireland. The Free State would ultimately become the Republic of Ireland with the six counties remaining part of the United Kingdom (Dwyer, 1998). The Civil War that followed was a conflict waged over the terms of the Anglo-Irish Treaty by Irish republicans (IRA) who opposed the treaty and rejected the imposition of a border on the island and Irish Nationalists (the provisional government of Ireland), who supported the treaty as a first step to later independence.

Throughout both wars, a central concern for the IRA was ensuring that the opposing side did not recruit spies or informers into their ranks (Murphy, 2011). Informers, spies, or touts played a very significant part in Irish republican history (Dudai, 2012) as a number of rebellions were thought to have failed due to the role of informers facilitating the enemy.

Importantly, informers featured prominently in public consciousness, and there was a widespread awareness of the depth of feeling regarding their folk devil status. In successive Irish revolutions, the rebel was deemed as the hero, whilst the informer was viewed with disdain, '*a symbol of evil since the days of penal law and priest hunters*' (Hart, 2009, p293).

To deter individuals from informing, the IRA proactively investigated suspected spies or informers often executing those found *guilty*; in some cases, they would be summarily executed and left at the roadside as a 'message' to other would-be informers (Keane, 2017). In other cases, individuals were simply disappeared and were never seen again. This campaign to identify and punish any such 'traitors' was pursued by the IRA within and across communities (Keane, 2017). The IRA was waging a war on two fronts—one against the British security forces, and a second against those in their own community whom they deemed to be working against them (Hart, 2009).

Whilst a complex range of issues may have led to disappearances, the prevailing reason given by republican paramilitaries was an allegation of spying or informing (O'Halpin, 2013). As mentioned above, the archetypal folk devil of the Irish revolution was the informer, and their abduction, execution and secret burial would appear to have been a tactic long practised (Fitzpatrick, 2013). The informer or spy, therefore, has huge strategic, and also emotive, significance for republicans (McMahon, 2008; O'Halpin, 2013; O'Ruairc, 2016). Due to the catastrophic impact of informers on prior rebellions, the IRA were exceptionally intolerant of any perceived betrayal and proactive in dealing with the issue (Dwyer, 1998).

Following a disappearance, a process of 'omerta' quickly descended onto an area, at a family, community and societal level (Fitzpatrick, 2013; Hart, 2009; Howe, 2014; Murphy, 2011; O'Halpin, 2013); this even extended to press coverage of the disappearance. Often, there was no acknowledgement of the violence in the local news. There were cases where the family placed advertisements in local newspapers asking for information regarding the abduction of a loved one, even though the abduction did not appear as an actual story anywhere in the newspaper (Murphy, 2011). This was thought to be the outcome of the all-encompassing control exerted by the IRA at the time, but also the power of the stigma attached to the label of informer.

The process of maintaining silence may also have been assisted by the exodus of families from Ireland following the abduction of their loved ones (Fitzpatrick, 2013; Hart, 2009; Murphy, 2011). But more likely is the fact that families colluded with the silence, fearful of inviting further IRA violence against them (Murphy, 2011). Even when families did contact the authorities, they too were silent, unhelpful and unresponsive (Hart, 2009). A complicating factor was that the nascent State stayed silent in an effort to maintain respectability around the IRA as some of its members were now senior figures in the Irish Government or in local authorities.

The IRA actively silenced families and communities, predominantly labelling the disappeared as spies to justify their behaviour. They threatened dire consequences should the victims' families inform anyone about their loved one's abduction or disappearance (Fitzpatrick, 2013; Howe, 2014; Keane, 2014; Murphy, 2011). There are reports that the Cork IRA responded very robustly to any enquiries regarding the whereabouts of civilians or members of the State forces abducted and killed, stating '*Those shot during the war, (are) not to be inquired about as they are all spies in this area*' O'Halpin (2013, p. 318). This rendered, not only the families but also whole communities silent.

Whilst understanding the disappearances that occurred during the Independence Conflict period in Ireland is vital to appreciating the cultural, political and community impact of the tactic, both at the time and in more recent years, disappearance as a tool of war has long been used in conflict zones around the world. The nuance of the Irish incidences of disappearance tells part of the story, but disappearance cannot be fully understood without considering it in the context of its wider international use. Disappearance creates tiers of victims, whereby the individuals, families and communities involved are all impacted by the act. In a sense it is public victimisation, an act of control and an act, not of repeat victimisation, but ongoing victimisation. As a result, the *harm*, particularly the psychological harm that reverberates from a disappearance, is highly relevant to understanding the impact of the act, regardless of the context.

Up until the end of World War II, the use of enforced disappearance as a weapon of war, although well known, was sparsely documented (Dulitizky, 2019b). However, since the mass disappearances of the Holocaust (Giorgou, 2013; Mentan, 2021), there has been sustained attention given to the tactic when used by States and paramilitaries alike.

Since WWII, hundreds of thousands of individuals have disappeared in conflicts around the world. It is estimated that, in more than 85 countries, enforced disappearance has been used as a means of control and of eliminating political opponents (Dewhirst & Kapur, 2015). Perhaps, due to the scale, the highest profile cases of individuals being disappeared are those involving the military dictatorships that governed many of the countries of Latin America from the 1950s to the 1980s. In Guatemala the military government disappeared between 40 to 50,000 people during the country's 36-year civil war (Peccerelli & Henderson, 2021). In Argentina, an estimated 30,000 individuals disappeared between 1976 and 1983, whilst, in Chile, approximately 3000 people vanished at the hands of General Augusto Pinochet's soldiers between 1973 and 1990 (Aguilar & Kovras, 2019). However, disappearing people has not been the preserve of Latin American dictators alone. In a number of cases, those disappeared were abducted and killed by either guerrilla/insurgent groups opposed to the regimes in power in the country in question, or by paramilitary groups sponsored by, or acting with, the acquiescence of the regime (Dulitizky, 2019b).

The United Nations (UN) has recognised the different players and methods involved in enforced disappearance. Article 2 of the 2006 International Convention for the Protection of All Persons from Enforced Disappearance (CED) United Nations (UN) (2006)—one of the 18 Human Rights Conventions that Member States are expected to ratify and abide by—defines enforced disappearance as:

> 'The arrest, detention, abduction or any other form of deprivation of liberty by agents of the State or by person or groups of persons acting with the authorisation, support or acquiescence of the State, followed by a refusal to acknowledge the deprivation of liberty or by concealment of the fate or whereabouts of the disappeared person, which place such a person outside the protection of the law'.

Article 3 adds that:

> 'Each State Party shall take appropriate measures to investigate acts defined in article 2 committed by persons or groups of persons acting without the authorization, support or acquiescence of the State and to bring those responsible to justice'.

Whilst the UN has recognised the involvement of groups other than corrupt regimes in enforced disappearances around the world, it is only recently that the literature on the practice of disappearance by insurgent or paramilitary groups has grown. Amongst the most well documented are the cases of Peru, Sri Lanka and Colombia, but recent examples from Syria, including the actions of the Islamic State of Iraq and Syria (ISIS), have been noted (Sarkin, 2021).

In Colombia, it is estimated that over 100,000 people were victims of enforced disappearance between 1958 and 2013, with over 62% carried out by paramilitaries, many in the final phase of the war (Cronin-Furman & Krystalli, 2020). In Peru, the figure is estimated to be in the region of 20,000 people disappeared between 1970 and 2000, the majority by insurgent and paramilitary groups (Garcia-Godos, 2013; Subramaniam et al., 2014). In Sri Lanka, there were over 70,000 enforced disappearances from the 1980s until relatively recently with State forces predominantly carrying out disappearances in the 1970s and 1980s, and insurgent and paramilitary groups intensifying the practice of enforced disappearance from the 1980s onwards (Harrison, 2013; Somasundaram, 2014). In all of these cases, there was substantial involvement by insurgents or guerrillas, and paramilitary groups (De Alwis, 2009; Haugaard & Nicholls, 2010; Subramaniam et al., 2014; Garcia-Godos, 2018; Dulitizky, 2019a; Berman-Arevalo, 2021). The common feature across all of these groups is that they operate on an intracommunity basis, submerged and intertwined across all aspects of community life.

Whilst at the individual family level, the impact of disappearance may appear obvious, it is important to note that the use of disappearances adds a level of complexity to a country's efforts to return to relative normality following a period of conflict. This relates to the legacy of the disappearance and its impact across generations, but also the secrecy and silence that particularly surround disappearances. In all cases, a central problem is the fact that the number of individuals to have suffered enforced disappearance can often only be estimated (De Alwis, 2009; Andreu-Guzman, 2012; Garcia-Godos, 2018; Bassel, 2019; Berman-Arevalo, 2021). There are often no official lists of those missing; (Cronin-Furham & Krystalli, 2020) there is also often a reluctance amongst medical and legal entities to investigate, report or record enforced disappearances (Haugaard & Nicholls, 2010) and/or in some cases, no legal requirement to record deaths or any associated medical or legal investigations. Political issues can also come into play (Humphreys, 2018), as, for example, in Colombia were not all of those disappeared were officially registered as disappeared due to the laws around who could be registered as a political victim

(Colombia Potencia De La Vida, 2018). There is also the issue of deniability, as is the case in Northern Ireland, where estimates of those who were disappeared are based solely on the admission of the perpetrators. This lack of record keeping, together with the absence of accountability, funerals and memorials was a successful way to ensure that there would be no public account of the social or political identity of an individual, and it was a useful strategy to erase the violence and, thereby, erase and eliminate the individual's standing and presence within their family and community (Alvarez, 2007).

Any family whose loved one has disappeared will have faced some or all of the difficulties outlined above in their pursuit of justice. However, when paramilitary, insurgent or guerrilla groups are responsible for enforced disappearance, there is an added burden for families. In many cases, the perpetrators are known to the families affected, and may live and work within the same community—individuals may share a space, identity or history with the perpetrators and, as a result, have the very jarring experience of being subjected to community rejection, identity denial and coercive control. The following chapters document this phenomenon as it occurred in the six counties of Northern Ireland.

REFERENCES

Aguilar, P., & Kovras, I. (2019). Explaining disappearances as a tool of political terror. *International Political Science Review, 40*(3), 437–452.

Alvarez, S. (2007). Disappearance (enforced), Crime against humanity. *Journal of International Criminal Justice, 5*(2), 480–492.

Andreu-Guzman, F. (2012). *Criminal justice and forced disappearance in colombia, Case studies on transitional justice; International commission for transitional justice.* Available at: https://www.brookings.edu/idp (Accessed: March 17 2017).

Bassel, H. (2019). Acts of truth telling and testimony in the conceptualisations of reparations in post conflict Peru. *Global Society, 34*(1), 84–98.

Berman-Arévalo, E. (2021). Mapping violent land orders: Armed conflict, Moral economies and the trajectories of land occupation and dispossession in the Colombian Caribbean. *The Journal of Peasant Studies, 48*(2), 349–367.

Bielenberg, A. & Donnelly, J. (2016). *Cork Spies Files: Suspected Spies and the Historical Evidence.* Available at: http://theirishrevolution.ie/cork-spy-files/#.WkZII00pXmI (Accessed: May 10 2017).

Bielenberg, A. & O'Ruairc, P. (2020a). Shallow graves: Documenting and assessing IRA disappearances during the Irish Revolution 1919–1923. *Small*

Wars and Insurgents. Available at: https://doi.org/10.1080/09592318. 2020.1798678 (Accessed: December 12 2021).

Borgonova, J. (2007). Spies. *Informers and the 'Anti Sein Fein' society; The intelligence war in Cork city 1920–1921.* Irish Academic Press.

Colombia Potencia De La Vida. (2018). *Single registry of victims* - https://www.unidadvictimas.gov.co/en/application-for-registration-in-the-single-registry-of-victims/ (Acessed January 6th 2020).

Cronin-Furman, K. & Krystalli, R. (2020). The things they carry: Victims' documentation of forced disappearance in Colombia and Sri Lanka. *European Journal of International Relations, 27*(1), 1–23. Available at: https://doi.org/10.1177/1354066120946479 (Accessed: December 18 2020).

De Alwis, M. (2009). Disappearance and displacement in Sri Lanka. *Journal of Refugee Studies, 22*(3), 378–391.

Dewhirst, P. & Kapur, A. (2015). The Disappeared and invisible. *Revealing the enduring impact of enforced disappearance on women.* International Center for Transitional Justice.

Dudai, R. (2012). Informers and the transition in Northern Ireland. *The British Journal of Criminology, 52*(1), 32–54.

Dulitizky, E. (2019a). Conceptualisation of reparation in post conflict Peru. *Global Society, 34*(1), 84–98.

Dulitizky, E. (2019b). The Latin-American Flavor of Enforced Disappearances Chicago. *Journal of International Law, 19*(2), pp. 423–489.

Dwyer, T. (1998). *Big fellow.* Gill and MacMillan Press.

Fitzpatrick, D. (2013). The Spectre of ethnic cleansing in revolutionary Ireland. In Roddie, R. (Ed.) *Bulletin of the methodist historical society* (Vol. 18, no. 18). Methodist Historical Society of Ireland.

Garcia-Godos, J. (2013). Victims rights and distributive justice: In search of actors. *Human Rights Rev, 14*(3), 241–255.

Garcia-Godos, J. (2018). Transitional justice in Peru: Lessons for Colombia'. In Pabon, F. (Ed.) *Truth, Justice and reconciliation in Colombia transitioning from violence.* Routledge.

Giorgou, I. (2013). State involvement in the perpetration of enforced disappearance and the Rome statute. *Journal for Criminal Justice, 11*, 1001–1021.

Harrison, F. (2013). *Still counting the dead.* Portobello Books.

Hart, P. (2009). *The IRA and its Enemies. Violence and community in cork 19161923.* Oxford University Press.

Haugaard, L. & Nicholls, K. (2010). *Breaking the silence in search of Colombia's disappeared.* Latin America Working Group Education Fund.

Howe, S. (2014). Killing in cork and the historians. *History Workshop Journal* 77. Available at: http://oxfordjournals.org (Accessed: March 2 2016).

Humphrey, M. (2018). The political lives of the Disappeared in the transition from conflict to peace in Colombia. *Religion and Ideology, 19*(4), 452–470.

Keane, B. (2014). *Massacre in West Cork*. Mercier Press.

Keane, F. (2017). *Wounds a memoir of war & love*. William Collins.

McMahon, P. (2008). *British Spies & Irish rebels. British intelligence and Ireland 1916–1945*. Boydell Press.

Mentan, T. (2021). *Ambacide: The genocide and extermination reminiscent of extermination of Jews (Holocaust) by Adolf Hitler*. RPCIG.

Murphy, G. (2011). *The year of disappearances. Political killings in Cork 1921–1922*. Gill Books.

O'Halpin, E. (2013). Problematic killings during the war of independence and its aftermath; Civilian spies and informers. In Kelly, J. & Lyons, M. (Eds.) *Death and dying in Ireland, Britain and Europe*. Sprintprint.

O'Ruairc, P. (2016). Truce. *Murder myth and the last days of the Irish War of independence*. Mercier Press.

Peccerelli, F. & Henderson, E. (2021). Forensics and maya ceremonies. The long journey for truth in Guatemala. In Brown, S. & Smith, S. (Eds.). *The routledge handbook of religion, Mass atrocity and genocide*. Routledge.

Sarkin, J. (2021). The need for a new paradigm in internal law to provide international protection. Protection: Learning the lessons from past processes and designing a mechanism to assist victims of arbitrary detentions of enforced disappearances in Syria. *International Human Rights Law Review, 10*(2), 247–290.

Somasundaram, D. (2014). *Scarred communities*. Psychosocial impact of man-made and natural disasters on Sri Lankan society.

Subramaniam, J., Majumder, N., Hatta, Z., & Zakari, A. (2014). Implications of enforced disappearances on women-headed families in the Northern province, Sri Lanka. *International Journal of Humanities and Social Science, 4*(4), 236–243.

United Nations. (2006). *International convention for the protection of all persons from enforced disappearance*. 47/133 Entry into force: 23 December 2010. In accordance with article 39(1), United Nations Human Rights. Office of the High Commissioner. Available at: https://treaties.un.org/pages/ViewDetails.aspx?src=TREATY&mtdsg_no=IV-16&chapter=4 (Accessed: January 12 2018).

Victims' Voices

Abstract The stories of the Disappeared are harrowing: the disappearance of sole parents leaving children orphaned, babies never having the chance to meet their fathers and families left broken. To compound the agony, several of the young men abducted had educational or learning difficulties, and were seen as very vulnerable by their families. From the moment of the abduction, the families carried this loss, often alone as it was too dangerous to talk about what had happened. The families' feelings of loss were intensified by the omnipresence of the paramilitaries in their community and the ravaging impact of the conflict that was going on around them. The families have waited, in some cases up to five decades, for the return of their loved one's bodies or for information about their murder and secret burial. They are still fighting for information and justice today. This chapter captures the voices of the families involved in this publication and explores their personal experiences of neglect, silence, blame and control and the hands of paramilitary organisations and the broader community.

Keywords Disappearance · Loss · Trauma · Silence · Fear · Unknown · Abduction · Secret burial

29

S. Peake and O. Lynch, *The Disappeared*, Palgrave Studies in Compromise after Conflict,
https://doi.org/10.1007/978-3-031-64713-0_4

The stories of the Disappeared are harrowing: the disappearance of sole parents leaving children orphaned, babies never having the chance to meet their fathers, and families left broken. To compound the agony, several of the young men abducted had educational or learning difficulties, and were seen as very vulnerable by their families. From the moment of the abduction, the families carried this loss, often alone as it was too dangerous to talk about what had happened. The families' feelings of loss were intensified by the omnipresence of the paramilitaries in their community and the ravaging impact of the conflict that was going on around them. The families have waited, in some cases up to five decades, for the return of their loved one's bodies or for information about their murder and secret burial. They are still fighting for information and justice today.

In speaking with the families involved, the overwhelming feeling associated with the disappearance is the cataclysmic nature of the event; the disappearances were all consuming and took over every aspect of their lives. For most, it was not an acute, one-off event but, rather evolved over days, months and even years. The families do not focus on a moment of trauma, but on a lifetime spent dealing with it. They speak of the ongoing horror of not knowing what happened to their loved one: the re-victimisation and repeat victimisation by the paramilitaries and the neglect and abandonment by their community, the State and the church. They talk about the marginalisation by their community, the labelling, the silence, the isolation and violence, and how this impacted every aspect of their lives.

This chapter presents the findings of the analysis of interviews conducted with the families of the Disappeared. The quotations are taken verbatim from the interview transcripts but are anonymised to protect the identity of the contributors; the letter Z is used for any mention of any of The Disappeared. All quotations have been approved for inclusion by the participants themselves. In order to inform the analysis presented here, this study uses a grounded theory approach with the sole purpose of allowing the voices of the families of the Disappeared to be foregrounded. Thirteen families of the Disappeared were represented in this study and 40 individuals participated in repeat interviews.[1] Ethical approval was secured from University College Cork Ireland and participant consent was re-sought to use the specific quotations included in this book.

---

[1] Refer to Appendix A.

DISAPPEARANCE AS A CATASTROPHIC EVOLUTION

Like everyone else who lived in Northern Ireland during the Troubles, the participants in this study never expected to be victims of the violence. Whilst they witnessed violence on the streets and knew people who had been touched directly, they never thought it would come to their door.

'I never dreamt he would die'.

This belief was compounded by the fact that very few of the families witnessed the disappearance of their loved ones. The fact that they were victims only emerged years and, for some, even decades, later as the details of the abduction and murder of their loved one became known. When the families talk about the disappearance, they are not talking about the moment of the event. Rather, they are talking about the lifetime since their loved one went missing, the sense of bewilderment and loss that has followed their family across generations and their silent abandonment by friends, family, community, colleagues and the State.

'*Nobody would have taken your side and stood beside you and said 'yes the IRA took this young man, he didn't do anything to deserve an execution'.*

Disappearances were not the only trauma to affect the immediate family. As it became apparent what had likely happened, the silent withdrawal of extended family members and friends was commonplace, often due to the complexities of existing loyalties within the republican movement in their community.

'*Daddy's cousins and people like that were very republican …and … they didn't come forward or help or be sympathetic because they too had this attitude, well you know he must have got his "just desserts".*

One explanation for these family dynamics was the omnipresent fear of retribution by paramilitary groups if there was any question of loyalty faltering, or any form of challenge issued. However, in many cases, issues of social and conflict identity, community loyalty and disbelief in the capacity of the paramilitary groups to engage in any form of *unjust* violence was the reality. As a result, the disappearance was not just a very personal or family trauma, it was a public trauma; a trauma that involved victimisation and re-victimisation by family, neighbours and broader society. It entailed the labelling of the family as traitors, informers, criminals, and fantasists. In addition, it served to isolate and exclude them from support networks, stripped them of their sense of belonging and identity and dehumanised their loved ones. Stigmatisation, withdrawal and victimisation didn't just present externally. In some cases, it emerged within immediate family units, causing resentment and huge division; it split families along ideological lines. This led to complicated dynamics and relationships that crossed generations. The loss became about so much more than the (suspected) death of a loved one. It became about the death of a family and a way of life.

Waiting for Return

In most cases, there were no witnesses to the disappearances—individuals simply vanished. The participants speak of how, when their loved ones went missing, the family assumed that they would return within hours or days when they were released by whoever had taken them. Only when it was confirmed that neither the police nor the army were holding their loved ones, did the families deduce that republican paramilitaries had to be involved—there was always hope that they would return. However, given the reputation and practices of local paramilitaries who operated as a quasi-police force, the families feared that their loved ones would likely return with injuries (Deglow, 2016). Summary justice by the paramilitaries was often undertaken as a form of policing and was used as punishment or deterrence for perceived antisocial behaviour, or for engaging in actions seen to undermine paramilitaries' authority or control (Napier et al., 2017).

This control by the paramilitaries was tolerated and, in many cases, welcomed within the community given the context of the violence at the time (Cavanagh, 1997). However, for the paramilitaries to maintain this authority, their justice system had to be perceived as being 'fair', with punishments being seen to fit the crimes; excessive punishments or 'rough justice' risked alienating the community (Cavanagh, 1997). Killing individuals without a very good reason would have been perceived as excessive by the community and risked undermining the authority of the paramilitaries. As a result, in cases where it was perceived there might not be community tolerance for violence, the victims had to literally disappear. This was illustrated quite starkly in the account from a legal case in 2019 involving the disappearance of Jean McConville, a widowed mother of 10 children, who was killed and secretly buried in 1972. Reports on the case highlighted that the accused was recorded as saying that Jean McConville was disappeared because '*they couldn't take the heat from throwing her on the streets*' (Moriarty, 2019). The implication was that this form of rough justice would not have been tolerated by the community.

'*It was a very silent issue; it comes back to the fear factor and the control that organisations had on communities. Nobody wanted to 'talk'.*

Whilst their loved ones were missing, the families were left in a state of limbo and uncertainty. They were afraid to speak, yet increasingly convinced that republican paramilitaries were responsible for the disappearance. One family member contends that not only was the family afraid to attribute blame, but the community was afraid too.

'*And they were afraid to say. 'Yes the IRA done it, or no they didn't do it'. No one knew, but then at the same time everyone knew. I knew after the first couple of days when he wasn't back and he wasn't released that he had to be dead cause he never would have been away, you could set your watch on him'.*

To compound the anxiety and feelings of helplessness, the families were unable to seek outside help because paramilitary *rules* forbade families from contacting the police service. As a result, the community around them remained steadfastly silent. Such was the influence and control exerted by the paramilitaries on the community, that the families feared that if they spoke out they could be inviting more violence against themselves (Napier et al., 2017).

'*You knew they knew, but nobody actually said what they knew'.*

The fear was compounded by the tight-knit nature of the republican communities in which many of the families lived (Dudai, 2011). Family members speak of the danger associated with speaking out and the reluctance of their parents to do so when they have other children to look after. As a result, families were left in a state of helplessness and fear:

'*It was nonsensical you know, he was just lifted off the face of the earth and gone for no reason'.*

Families describe how, in the aftermath of the disappearances, the paramilitaries closed ranks and intimidated witnesses to prevent information from being shared. In a small number of cases where the family witnessed the kidnapping, they talk about how knowing that their loved one had been taken by PIRA, whilst deeply traumatic, helped the family fight against the repeated denials of involvement by the perpetrators and their efforts at obfuscation and misinformation.

'We were there to see our Z being taken away - I don't know whether you would call it lucky or not that we were there when it happened... Because if we hadn't seen our Z being taken away, we would have believed ....all the stories people were telling us; that's what would have happened. You would have believed that Z had run away so you would have'.

Regardless, of the families' efforts to fight against this misinformation, it still served to muddy the waters enough to isolate the family and ensure some degree of deniability by PIRA; this prevented the community and even the police from taking the issue seriously. This sense of being controlled was felt by the familes as an *orchestrated* process which ensured that not only did they have to deal with the disappearance, but, they also had to suffer 'gaslighting' by their extended families and friends, by their community, and by agents of the State (Somasundaram et al., 2011).

'People would have said very negative things like "He deserved it," or "Hell roast him". There was like a message that he deserved it and it was to control us definitely'.

The isolation and lack of information led to a deep sense of despair and, in a number of cases where the families suspected what had happened, led them to take on physical searches themselves. A harrowing account by one mother mirrors the testimonies of other participants who were desperate to locate their loved one's body but were faced with a wall of silence when trying to get information on where, or if, their remains had been secretly buried.

'I used to go away up the fields in the early hours of the morning on my own and dig through the soil looking for his body because I knew he was dead'.

The response of the community went beyond simply ignoring the family. It was felt as an active process in which support and 'neighbourliness' were withdrawn. Family members recall that they were treated as 'undesirable' and a wall of silence was erected around them. Isolation and a sense that they were on their own from the day of the abduction until the recovery of the remains, was an experience common to all of the families.

The families felt that the nature of the isolation and abandonment they experienced was unique to victims of disappearance and that the identity of the perpetrator was particularly relevant to their experience. As Catholic victims of the PIRA, the Disappeared were not treated like other victims; they were seen to be less worthy of sympathy and more likely to be blamed for their own fate. Violence by the *other side* was treated completely differently: troubles related incidents involving loyalists or the State were treated as a violation of the whole community. There was a sense of vicarious victimhood for *all* members of that community and this was publicly acknowledged (Manktelow, 2007). Across Nationalist communities, help and support were actively and visibly provided to individual victims and families who had experienced loss at the hands of loyalist paramilitaries, the police or army.

'My poor mother. Not one rapped the door to say 'Mrs (surname) are you all right?''

This demonisation of the family members was not short-lived. For many individuals, it lasted up to the point in 1999 when the PIRA/INLA lists confirmed that a number of the missing were disappeared. For others, it lasted right up to the time of the recovery of their loved one's body.

The Emergence of Community Shame

Due to the marginalisation, isolation and a sense of abandonment felt by the families of the Disappeared, for a long time, they believed that they were the only such victims.

'I couldn't believe after reading the newspaper that all them people were disappeared, I couldn't believe it. I thought it was only our Z, I suppose they all thought the same'.

The family members noticed a perceptible shift in attitude amongst their community once the truth started emerging about disappearances. The trigger in some cases was the recovery of the body whilst, for others, it was the acknowledgement by PIRA or INLA that the person had in fact been disappeared. For the participants in this study, the behaviour of extended families and communities in the aftermath of the initial disappearance was understood as a reaction to the misinformation promulgated by the paramilitary groups, their supporters and others.[2]

'I think a lot of them, in the beginning they would have seen the people who disappeared as problem people. Who needed to, let's say, who needed to be disappeared. So therefore, they found justification in their thinking for that'.

There was a perceptible shift in how the community behaved once the fate of the victims became known; in most cases, the community responded with shame and guilt.

'Before the funeral finally arrived, you were able to open up and talk to people you weren't able to talk to before and people were apologising and saying 'I would have loved to have said something to you, but I was afraid'.

However, the recovery of bodies, or the admission of guilt by the paramilitaries presented a challenge to both the communities and the perpetrators. Apart from the initial violence associated with the abduction and killing, for the families, the sustained effort to hide the disappearance for so many years had exposed both the duplicity of the paramilitary group, and the extent to which its members had orchestrated, both the initial violent act, and the suffering of the families in the aftermath. As a result of the admission that individuals had been disappeared and the subsequent recovery of some of the bodies, the families believe there was a shift to what they referred to as a 'process of community shame'.

'People were disgusted when they realised really what they [paramilitaries] did, people were shocked, it was hard to believe how shocked the whole community could be, that was so republican minded and listened to everything they

---

[2] See for example the Police (PSNI) Ombudsman report into the disappearance of Jean Mc Conville https://cain.ulster.ac.uk/issues/police/ombudsman/po130806.pdf.

were told and agreed with everything they were told [by the paramilitaries], and then for this to come up'.

'There's a lot of people around here disgusted at what they've done. People came to me when they found out that Z was one of the Disappeared: "That should never have happened"'.

The emergence of community shame was an inversion of the experiences of the families up to that point. During the period of searching and truth seeking, there was a sense that the shame rested solely with the families. Until this point shame had permeated all aspects of their lives rendering them marginalised; after this point, it became a public shame.

'In a lot of ways, you sort of held your head down, you sort of couldn't hold your head up. You were conscious all the time of what people were saying behind your back, what people were thinking but what they weren't saying. That's how I felt , you know going up the town afterwards and going to meet people afterwards, I felt that...I was sort of keeping me head down with shame'.

VICTIM BLAMING

For many years those who perpetrated the disappearances in Northern Ireland denied any involvement—the families speak of how the perpetrators promoted a narrative that the victims had in some way been responsible for their own abduction and death. In the *hierarchy of victims,* those labelled as informers and killed by paramilitaries from their own community were perceived to be the lowest of the low (McEvoy & McConachie, 2013). Their deaths were often not recognised or remembered by anyone associated with, or sympathetic to, the respective paramilitary groups; a phenomenon widely witnessed in other jurisdictions abroad (Haugaard & Nicholls, 2010; Nicholls, 2010; Weliamuna, 2012).

'Obviously there is a stigma attached with a Catholic being killed by the Provisionals, you know what I mean'.

The impact of this was stark as it rendered community support non-existent.

'You still have that stigma. It still goes back to that stigmatisation of I don't want to get involved in this because this involves paramilitaries and we don't want to bring trouble'.

By branding their loved ones as informers, known by the colloquial term 'tout', the republican paramilitaries characterised the victims as not only having betrayed the republican movement, but also the community in which they lived (Dudai, 2011).

'Well they [the Disappeared] were all branded as touts weren't they and being a tout was like the worst thing you could be'.
  'When the IRA kill somebody they brand them with a label such as an informer, which is one of the worst things ever'.
  'Because you say oh the IRA killed him, so they say well he must have been in the IRA. They judge so it's easier just to say nothing, and not mention it'.

As well as feeling belittled in the eyes of the community, the families were equally challenged by the assertion that their loved ones' own actions had caused them to be disappeared.

'So the neighbours didn't really openly offer any sympathy, you know they just kind of shrugged their shoulders and nodded their heads as if to say well 'maybe he got you know what he deserved'.
  'I think that is really why a lot of people think, I think, they would say "och sure he was mixed up and he deserved all he got", you know all that, horrible people'.

In addition, for the families, there was a perception that there was less assistance offered by paramilitaries in locating the bodies of a loved one if the victim had been associated with the paramilitary organisation. There was an inherent assumption within communities that, when the paramilitaries killed members of their own community, they were justified in doing so (Knox, 2002). This arose because of a belief within the community that the paramilitaries were acting in the community's best interest; their denials or later statements on the Disappeared were, therefore, believed.

'They kind of kept looking out of the sides of their eyes, because anyone who went missing, well not so much went missing in those days but who were punished because of crimes against the IRA you know, nobody would sympathise with you'.

In Fig. 4.1. The power of the stigma linked to being an *informer* perpetuated the isolation and marginalisation of families and rendered them even more powerless, compounding their feelings of injustice.

'They still keep saying Z was an informer, and stuff like this here. That's what pisses me off the most when you know that Z wasn't'.

The sense that this could bring further harm to the family was felt strongly by some and, in some cases, individuals even began to wonder if the misinformation might actually be true.

'I thought that maybe that he had informed. And if that was the case, well then you did keep your mouth shut because you would have been afraid to get yourself involved in that'.

'You're afraid... if Z has done something, that's going to make us guilty as well, so you are a bit nervous about going places'.

Fig. 4.1 Graffiti on the Divis Flats in West Belfast in 1979. Photograph ©Brendan Murphy

The doubt, coupled with an ongoing fear, led families to further retreat from the community. It also led to a deepening silence and, ultimately, to the further degradation of the memories of their disappeared loved ones.

SILENCE

The degradation of the memories of their loved ones, even years after the disappearance, created a toxic environment for the families. There was a sense throughout the interviews that families were trapped, unable to leave the area in which they lived, and unable to escape the situation. Initially, families stayed in their areas as a number were concerned that their loved ones might return and not be able to find them. Others were afraid to leave for fear of drawing further attention, threats or even violence.

'The republicans who disappeared people just wanted to wipe you out - your whole memory - they didn't want you to be remembered'.

'Oh, you better want to watch yourself or you will get the same as what your brother got'.

Age was no barrier to taunting or violence. Even as children, the participants were singled out.

'We were treated like scum, we were, we were treated like scum, we got spat in our faces, told that Z ran off... told us that Z didn't want us no longer'.

These were deeply painful recollections and, even today, family members continue to see some of the people who taunted and even attacked them within their neighbourhood. The families feel that the victimisation was and is compounded by the fact that the perpetrators still show no remorse for their actions.

'To me we got the raw end of the stick from the word go in this and we are still getting it'.

However, it was not only the neighbours who abandoned the families, the silence of key institutions, such as the medical and legal fraternities, social services and the Church, also caused the families additional suffering for decades. For the families in the study, there was a general sense that none of these practitioners or agencies gave any credence to the issue of the disappearance nor offered any support to the families.

'We didn't know anything about social services. Nobody helped us, not a sinner'.

The fact that these agencies did not help or give a public voice to the experiences of the families allowed them to be further victimised, and then re-victimised, over the years. Part of this repeat cycle of victimisation was the demonisation of family members. They were regarded as being toxic and, as a result, they were viewed as untouchable. This led to their ostracisation, not only within their own local community but even in their workplaces. The victimisation did not abate with time, in some cases, it continues to impact the families to this day.

'Even when we got to the age of working.... if you were working on a building site and the IRA found out you were working on the building site, and knew you, they used to say to the foreman, "I don't want him working there". Then he would have to tell you there was no work there for you. This was happening all the time'.
'At times you couldn't get a job, because of who you are'.

The power that republican paramilitaries had within the community was far reaching. As a result, in order to survive, the families adopted strategies to maintain a low profile in work and within the community, not speaking about their loved one who had disappeared and emphasising the respectability of the family.

'The families had to develop a shield around them to protect themselves from that outer ring of condemnation'.

Whilst the 1999 statement brought a number of the cases out into the public arena, some family members were still reluctant to lobby publicly for the return of the remains.

'To be honest, I didn't want to become known in work as one of the families of the Disappeared'.
'I worked in a factory and I travelled around customers all over the North of Ireland and the South, aye, you just had to be anonymous, everywhere and as quiet as could be, there was no references to anything whatsoever'.

As well as dealing with negative responses from their own community the families had to protect themselves from the reaction of the unionist/loyalist community. The fact that their loved one had disappeared meant there was an assumption that their family was somehow associated with the PIRA/ INLA. This meant that families always had to be careful about how they engaged with those outside their community, including in the workplace.

'All sorts of customers, all places that I had to keep a low profile'.

PROTECTORS, ENFORCERS AND PERPETRATORS

For the families, republican paramilitaries were viewed as having three central functions: protectors, enforcers and perpetrators. The significance of each of these roles can be traced back to the developmental trajectory of the paramilitary organisations within communities. As protectors, the participants in the study spoke of how the paramilitaries were the rulers of the community adopting the role of a quasi-police force.

'They were supposed to be the army in the streets… if you heard anybody, something going wrong, something, you went to them ones… you sort of looked to them cause they were the rulers of the land, you know'.

This role of paramilitaries as protectors was not just for protection against the actions of loyalists or State forces; it was also to ensure intra-community control. Behaviour that was perceived as antisocial, or that challenged the paramilitaries' authority, was proactively addressed. Transgressions were subjected to a variety of punishments, including violent assaults (known as punishment beatings), abduction and interrogation, shooting through the knees (known as kneecapping) and expulsion into exile (Kennedy, 2020; Napier et al., 2017). One family member noted that the paramilitaries grew to be perceived as the community 'rulers' and that this had emerged in part because of a policing vacuum given that the RUC were not visible or welcome in the community. As a result, if you needed a problem sorted out, the only option was to go to 'the boys', to get it resolved (Dudai, 2012).

Whilst the ultimate aim of this violence was to exert and maintain control and ensure discipline within the community, it was also intended to achieve the same result within the paramilitary organisation itself

(Morrison, 2016). In addition, intracommunity discipline often satisfied community members' demands for retribution when they had been harmed, which, in turn, endorsed the paramilitaries' role as community protectors (McEvoy, 2003). Given the omnipresent threat of violence, the community members were always aware of the consequences of *stepping out of line*.

> *"That's part of the thing they did, they (paramilitaries) kept you under control".*
>
> *'I think they (the IRA) owned the place, they were the bullies and I think if they didn't like something… they were quick to bump somebody off. You know it hadn't to be that bad'.*
>
> *'Z was shot in the back of the head, you know it was judge and jury, bang bang and buried in a bog in the back arse hole of nowhere, with no one'.*

Whilst there was no external accountability or sanction against the PIRA, the paramilitaries knew that there was a balance to be struck; they understood that they risked alienating the community if their violence was considered unjustified, or perceived as rough justice (Cavanagh, 1997). However, the role of the paramilitaries was not just policing the communities, it was also controlling the communities and this included managing the aftermath of the disappearances by keeping the families in line.

One family member explained that they could not be seen at the house of another family whose loved one had been disappeared. They perceived that there was active monitoring of their activities and that this was intended to promote a climate of fear and ensure control was maintained. As a result, families felt that republican paramilitaries were not solely fighting the oppression of the British State forces, rather they had also become oppressors within their own community.

> *'Fear, fear seemed to be the biggest thing because it wasn't Catholic, Protestant, it was just them [IRA] and us. We were repressed, and they ruled you, you were repressed like, you were kept down, and things would happen and you couldn't say 'God, that was wrong, that was terrible', cause you could have been taken away anywhere. It was just the way people lived at the time; it's hard to explain that to someone who didn't live through it'.*

The fear was palpable; there was a continuous watchfulness amongst the families and often they felt unable to speak openly until they were outside their area, or deemed themselves to be in a safe place. This sense of fear, compounded feelings of powerlessness; some commented on how this lasted for decades.

> *'You would talk to no outsiders [be]cause you didn't know who was in your favour'.*
>
> *'I was working in a bar that time and that's when I got the gun to the head and told to keep quiet'.*

It is striking that despite the Peace Process and ceasefires, the paramilitaries still remained as threatening as ever for the families of the Disappeared. To some extent, this continues even now, over twenty-five years after the Good Friday Agreement (GFA). It was noted across the interviews that the families continued to have to moderate what they said or did because of the local presence of those who were thought to be involved, or who might still be involved with republican paramilitaries. This has been exacerbated by the legacy caused by living under continuous threat (Smid et al., 2020), in which the longevity of the emotional trauma hasn't abated even with the recovery of the remains of their loved ones.

FOLLOWING THE RULES—GROWING UP IN NORTHERN IRELAND

'Whatever you say, Say Nothing' (Heaney, 1975, p10).

The title of Seamus Heaney's poem reflects how the participants in this study lived their lives. Throughout the interviews, they spoke of how they learned the rules of engagement from an early age. Children were encouraged not to look at, speak to, or engage with the army because of the danger it could bring from paramilitaries.

> *'If the army were going around the street and the children were looking out the window at them, he'd [father] scowl and he say "mind your own business and keep to yourself, don't be looking out there at them" '.*

The British Army and the RUC were the enemy. It followed that if an individual witnessed any paramilitary activity within the community they would not report it; if they heard anything, it would not be repeated.

These were the rules associated with day-to-day life for both sides of the community throughout the Conflict.

> *'Me father would have said, say nothing, see nothing, hear nothing, know nothing and that's the way it went on for years'.*
>
> *'In the 80's and 90's you kept yourself to yourself, you seen nothing, you heard nothing, you know nothing…because you don't want to be bringing trouble on yourself or your family you know. People would just get on with their work and say nothing'.*

Often individuals were sent to warn family members that they should not engage with the authorities; there was a fear that this might impact, not only on them, but also on the community in which they lived.

> *'One neighbour came up to the house at one stage and said to my mother not to bring the police into the area, for her sake and their sake'.*

For the families of the Disappeared these rules were particularly prominent, as were the consequences of being seen not to follow them.

> *'You had to protect yourself and protect your own people, or protect your family, so you didn't go against, you know, the grain. It was almost as though you had to accept your fate and you got on with it, and you know, how dare you, you know kick up about it'.*

The result of this situation was that individuals felt unable to fight back against what had happened—they felt that they had to accept it and get on with life, regardless of the fate of their loved one. The ripple effect of these rules was that individuals wouldn't even speak openly in their own home. The omnipresence of paramilitary groups, and the secrecy around who was involved in the organisations, led to a continual state of watchfulness and adherence to the imposed silence even within the apparent safety of their own homes.

> *'Like any talk we ever did we had to whisper, they used to put things to the window and listen in, so you couldn't, you could never have a conversation'.*
>
> *'I didn't feel happy, I didn't feel, I, I was always looking over my shoulder'.*

The legacy of these rules of engagement permeated individuals' lives leaving a lasting sense of unease, particularly for those whose loved ones' remains have not yet been recovered. They still feel a crushing sense of control over their lives.

CONTROLLING THE NARRATIVE
AND OBSTRUCTING THE TRUTH

The families felt that their day-to-day lives were being controlled. A key part of this was the extent to which the paramilitaries were able to control the narrative around disappearances and the Disappeared themselves. The use of false narratives, whereby stories and rumours were manufactured to imply that the individuals were still alive, or to deny they were dead were experienced by many family members.

> 'In the first few years you'd never think he is dead. Stories were put out that he was seen in England, he's away to America or Australia'.

Throughout this study, a variety of narratives were shared that had emerged to explain the disappearances: that the victim had left of their own free will because they no longer wanted to be with their wife or their family, that they had joined the circus or the army, or travelled abroad, or that they had done something so bad they deserved to fade into oblivion. This was a common theme in other conflicts featuring enforced disappearances; individuals were deemed to be amoral, and certainly not 'ideal' or innocent victims due to some assumption that they precipitated their own fate (Christie, 1986; Hussain, 2019; Isuru et al., 2019; Koc-Menard, 2014; Martinez, 2013; Nicholls, 2010).

> 'You would always hear the rumour mill that... they have ran here, they have ran away there. I don't think people actually knew the enormity of what actually had happened'.
> 'They put out messages that he's away to America or that... he rued his marriage. You knew that wasn't right'.

Controlling the narrative about the Disappeared through an orchestrated process enabled the truth to be obscured. Many of the interviewees reported that this was extremely hurtful as the stories were often focused on the families left behind.

> 'All that did was create hurt for us'.

These stories were not just occasional; new information, new sightings and speculation emerged over and over. One of the participants concluded that the paramilitaries must have had a series of individuals acting as 'planters', and that these 'planters' had orchestrated the stories. This misinformation served to limit questions from the community because they likely believed some or all of the messages. Cruelly, it also maintained a sense of hope for the families that their loved ones might still be alive. In one case a family received a Christmas card reputedly from their loved one.

> 'The Christmas after he had gone... we received a Christmas card through the post and it didn't have a postmark on it or anything and it was written to Mr and Mrs... It was very childish looking writing and Z wasn't a great writer, he would have written in a childish manner and... to us (this was) a sign that he was somewhere else and he was trying to contact us... that was like a little ray of hope'.

Families also received letters and confirmations of job applications all of which were designed to make them believe that their loved one was alive. In order to counteract the community unease, even the media were used—it was not unknown, for example, for a staged photograph of someone else to be printed, in order to suggest that an individual missing had returned to the community. The vulnerability and marginalisation of the family, compounded by silence and fear, meant that they had no allies to help them fight against this rhetoric or even to determine if it was true.

> 'Then you are desperate you know, you clutch at anything and to us, that in fact he is somewhere, somewhere still and he is not allowed to contact us and this (card) is his way of telling us that he is still here. And we grasped on to that for a long, long time and we never, ever did get to the bottom of it'.

The misinformation continued even after the PIRA admitted to engaging in enforced disappearances. For example, conflicting information was given to the families regarding where their loved ones were buried. This inaccurate information was highly traumatic for the families given their desperation to find their bodies.

> 'We got phone calls to say that Z was buried under a house... I used to be standing physically sick thinking how are they ever going to find him if he's buried under concrete'.

> *'Z was supposed to be buried under that motorway there, the Westlink [a motorway]. And all this, getting letters sent to the priest with like a wee map. Sent a map, aye, this is where Z was buried'.*

In some cases, the families' desperation, combined with the lack of police investigation or engagement, led families to search the areas themselves or to have areas searched at their own expense.

> *'If we heard anything at all, we would follow it up'.*

Letters and maps forwarded to priests, the media or anonymously to the family brought hope, but also huge distress. It was subsequently discovered that many of these reported burial sites were false and families felt that this was part of yet another process aimed at obstructing recovery. The families felt that they had to keep searching out of loyalty to their loved ones, or to their parents who had died in the intervening years.

> *'My daddy would still be throwing stones, pulling over in ditches, even down south like because they were feeding him a lot of nonsense and he was going to get the bottom of it no matter what. So if we hadn't found Z, my daddy would still be going. He would have paid for (named) dam to be drained, and then somewhere else and somewhere else and somewhere else… So when was he ever going to run out steam?'*

The power of the story of the Disappeared was evidenced by the efforts made to silence and deceive the families. The families represented a dissenting voice; they and their actions were a constant reminder of the brutality and rough justice meted out to ordinary and often vulnerable citizens during the Troubles. In addition, the participants believed that a key reason for controlling the narrative regarding the Disappeared was that they had significant potential to damage how the republican paramilitaries were perceived by their own community.

> *'They would be afraid they would lose a lot of support, which they would at that time'.*
> *'They didn't want to disclose this. They tried to protect themselves and their image. They still do so'.*

Controlling the narrative was therefore seen as part of a process of managing, not only the families and the community but also the reputation of the paramilitary group amongst its own community. This, along with a strategy of enforced silence or omerta around the Disappeared contributed to the families experiencing extreme and coercive control. Through a process which started at the moment of abduction, the families felt that the perpetrators had an ongoing direct and detrimental impact on the families left behind, compounding and freezing their grief, their access to any form of justice and facilitating their betrayal.

References

Cavanagh, K. (1997). Interpretations of political violence in ethnically divided societies. *Terrorism and Political Violence, 9*(3), 33–54.

Christie, N. (1986). The ideal victim. In Fattah, E. (Ed.) *From crime policy to victim policy*. Palgrave Macmillan.

Deglow, A. (2016). Localized legacies of civil war: Postwar violent crime in Northern Ireland. *Journal of Peace Research, 53*(6), 786–799.

Dudai, R. (2011). Closing the gap: Symbolic reparations and armed groups. *International Review of the Red Cross, 93*(883), 703–806.

Dudai, R. (2012). Informers and the transition in Northern Ireland. *The British Journal of Criminology, 52*(1), 32–54.

Haugaard, L. & Nicholls, K. (2010). *Breaking the silence in search of Colombia's disappeared*. Latin America Working Group Education Fund.

Heaney, S. (1975). *North*. Faber & Faber.

Hussain, S. (2019). Violence, Law and the archive: How dossiers of memory challenge enforced disappearances in the war on terror in Pakistan. *Political and Legal Anthropology Review, 42*(1), 53–67.

Isuru, A., Hewage, S., Padmakumara, P., & Williams, S. (2019). Unconfirmed death as a predictor of psychological morbidity in family members of disappeared persons. *Psychological Medicine, 49*(16), 2764–2771.

Kennedy, L. (2020). *Who was responsible for the troubles?* McGill Press.

Knox, C. (2002). See no evil, Hear no evil. *British Journal of Criminology, 42*(1), 164–185.

Koc-Menard, N. (2014). Notes from the field: Exhuming the past after the Peruvian internal conflict. *The International Journal of Transitional Justice, 8*(2), 277–299.

Manktelow, R. (2007). The needs of victims of the troubles in Northern Ireland: The social work contribution. *Journal of Social Work, 7*(1), 31–50.

Martinez, M. (2013). *Peru's painful mirror. Ten years after the final report, Peruvians reflect on the impact of the truth and reconciliation commission.* ICTJ.

McEvoy, K., & McConachie, K. (2013). Victims and transitional justice: Voice, Agency and blame. *Social & Legal Studies, 22*(4), 489–513.

McEvoy, K. (2003). Beyond the metaphor: Political violence, Human rights and new peacebuilding criminology. *Theoretical Criminology, 7*(3), 319–346.

Moriarty, G. (2019). Jean McConville's murder, the Boston tapes, Gerry Adams and the Ivor Bell trial. *Irish Times.* 17 October. Available at: https://www.iri shtimes.com/news/ireland/irish-news/jean-mcconville-s-murder-the-boston-tapes-gerry-adams-and-the-ivor-bell-trial-1.4053933 (Accessed: December 1 2021).

Morrison, J. (2016). Fighting talk: The statement of the IRA/New IRA. *Terrorism and Political Violence, 28*(3), 598–619.

Napier, R., Gallagher, B., & Wilson, D. (2017). An imperfect peace: Trends in paramilitary related violence 20 years after the northern ireland ceasefires. *Ulster Medical Journal, 86*(2), 99–102.

Nicholls, K. (2010). In search of Columba's disappeared. *The Guardian.* Available at: https://www.theguardian.com/global-development/poverty-matters/2010/dec/09/colombia-disappeared (Accessed: May 18 2018).

Smid, G., Blaauw, M., & Lenferink, L. (2020). Relatives of enforced disappeared persons in mexico: Identifying mental health and psychosocial support needs and exploring barriers to care intervention. *Journal of Mental Health and Psychosocial Support in Conflict Affected Areas, 18*(2), 139–149.

Somasundaram, D., Gooneratne, I., Pathirane, T., Dharmadasa, V. & Anonymous Author. (2011). Individual, Familial and social impacts of enforced disappearances. practices of a repressive ecology and ways of responding. In Lauritsch. K. & Kernjak, F. (Eds.). *We need the truth: Enforced disappearances in Asia.* ECAP.

Weliamuna, J. (2012). Discovering the white van in a troubled democracy. An analysis of ongoing abduction blueprint in Sri Lanka. *Groundviews.* Available at: https://groundviews.org/2012/04/28/discovering-the-white-van-in-a-troubled-democracy-an-analysis-of-ongoing-abduction-blueprint-in-sri-lanka/ (Accessed: April 15 2018).

CHAPTER 5

Activism Across
the Generations—An Awakening

Abstract For the families of the Disappeared, the legacy of the disappearance and its impact on family life was immense. The effect of the disappearance of a loved one was not just restricted to those who were old enough to have cognisance of the significance of the event at the time. For the individuals who participated in this study, it was evident that the disappearance had a profound effect across the second and even third generations. Fear was a constant companion across the generations. Part of the process of control in the aftermath of the violence was to increase fear and threaten anyone who spoke out. Overcoming this fear, taking up an activist role, and seeking justice for their loved ones was a part of the journey for the families in this volume. This chapter tracks this process and explores the trauma inflicted on the families across generations as they sought information on the disappearance of their family member.

Keywords Disappearance · Legacy · Transgenerational · Fear · Control · Threat · Activism

For the families of the Disappeared, the legacy of the disappearance and its impact on family life was immense. In many cases, it manifested in the break-up of the family unit.

> *'It (the disappearance) destroyed her (Mum), she destroyed us'.*

All of the participants reflected on the fact that life was never the same following the abduction—there had been a full life before their loved one was taken and, for many, a 'half-life' afterwards.

> *'I think that my Mum unfortunately constantly looks back, constantly looks back to the time in her life when she had Z and how perfect life was and then how her life you know half ended on (date)'.*

This 'half-life' was defined by the years of uncertainty regarding the fate of their loved ones—it was a time when they lived in a constant state of ambiguity. This became a marker of the schism between life as it was, and life after the abduction.

> *'As a family unit, we were split up and we were broke up, and we never became a family after it. That ended our family life as we knew it like, and we just grew up not really knowing each other'.*

Whilst some never regained an intact family unit, others attempted to come together in an effort to bolster the family, provide stability and cohesion, and search for their loved one. Most often the female lead in the household took on this role, providing stability, guidance and security for the children. Some family members were drawn closer into the family unit in an effort to buffer the negative effects of the traumatic loss, and as a means of dealing with threats from outside the family.

In addition to these roles, advocacy for their missing relative became a central focus for some family members, and by the mid-1990s, spokespeople started to emerge from within each family. Understandably, this was not a role the family members relished, and for the individuals involved, a sense of obligation was commonplace. The early spokespeople were nearly all female: the mothers, wives, daughters and siblings of the Disappeared. As well as providing emotional and practical support for their families, these women felt compelled to also adopt a public lobbying role. However, even in the late 1990s, the women were reluctant to be photographed, and as on the cover of this book, the pictures taken often excluded their faces—such was the fear of antagonising the paramilitaries within their local community.

For the families, when recovery came, they were able to lay their loved one to rest, however, family issues were often not laid to rest and, in several cases, these emerged with intensity, with family loyalties severely tested post-recovery. Just as grief had been contained as a form of survival, it was highlighted by some participants that issues bottled up over the years started to emerge when it was *all over*.

> *'It was an awful position to be in and that's when the family started to fall apart when he was found. It really got to you then that was the time you could change from being glad you had him, to being angry or wanting answers, that was the time you could see the change on the family. I could see it affecting the boys then, each one was different, each one it affected them differently'.*
>
> *'When you think what had happened it should have made the family stronger together, but it didn't - it just ripped us apart'.*

The recovery of the bodies by the ICLVR started a process for some families in which the legacy of the disappearance really came to the fore. The grief that had been frozen for years suddenly emerged; questions of injustice arose; questions regarding the reason for the disappearance emerged; and the lack of investigation and accountability really hit home. The sense of injustice also impacted on the next generation. In other conflicts the emotional cost of disappearance also became particularly intensified post-recovery and, similarly, challenges and difficulties for individuals and their families often deepened at that point (Salih & Samarasinghe, 2017).

> *'I am not degrading my Z or any of the other disappeared but once that bullet went into their head, they ceased to exist, nothing that they (the paramilitaries) could do, could hurt them ever again. It couldn't. So this was left to generations of families who are hurting for 40 years. Well they didn't do anything. Neither did the person that was shot, they didn't deserve it, but their families deserved it less'.*

In many cases, even after recovery, many of the participants recalled that they were unable to let the disappearance go; they had to continue to fight for the legacy of their loved one and support the rest of the families who continued to search for their loved ones remains.

Intergenerational Trauma

The effect of the disappearance of a loved one was not just restricted to those who were old enough to have cognisance of the significance of the event at the time. For the individuals who participated in this study, it was evident that the disappearance had a profound effect across the second and even third generations.

> 'I don't even want to touch it, only I'm embedded, it's a family thing. I wouldn't want to go near, but it's just, it was one of those really, really shady, shameful, disgusting things, that happened, that you just can't justify'.

Not wanting to deal with the issue, but feeling that it was embedded within the family history, reinforced a sense of responsibility to continue fighting for the recovery of a loved one. However, the fear and feeling of being controlled by an orchestrated campaign against them has applied as much to the younger generations as it did to older members of the family. This was particularly the case for children who remained living in the area, within the same social, recreational and educational structures as their parents. Family members have spoken of the effect of the ongoing stigmatisation and the underlying feeling of threat that remained years later due to the proximity of those responsible.

Whilst second and third generations of families eventually took up the role of spokesperson or advocate for their disappeared relative, somewhat ironically, they have also spoken about the silence surrounding the violence within their own family. The participants noted that, whilst there was a silence within the family, the issue was often palpable, even for children.

> 'The disappearance of my uncle came on the news and I remember my granny taking very ill'.
>
> 'The picture (of the young man disappeared) was there, but you would see her (Granny), when we came in from school, she would put out our dinner, she would go sit in her chair underneath his picture and just she would cry and we wouldn't know why, it was, and that was tough, she would say his name'.

Receiving only partial information, the children were often left with an incomplete picture. As a result, misinformation often took the place of facts, increasing fear and perpetuating the trauma of the loss; often myths became reality.

> 'We always thought, we kinda knew, he had been kidnapped but not politically, we just thought it was a random kidnapping, We used to walk home from school, home from Granny's. I remember looking over my shoulder thinking are we going to get kidnapped, cause he was kidnapped'.

In many cases the silence was thought to protect the younger generations—some felt they were sparing their children from the distress associated with the loss.

> 'We always made sure that they [the children] were safe and they didn't need to be weighed down by this problem'.
> 'Like I know I had a young family at the time and I never discussed anything with them because I was afraid that they would, that, it would come back on them'.
> 'So would I want them to carry on in this? No, no, no, I want them to live their lives and have hope and live it in peace and to bring my grandchildren up that they never have to face this'.

However, this was a traumatic way for any child to live; it made the world a more threatening place and intensified fear and distress. Whilst the intention was to protect the children, the secrecy in fact increased the terror and uncertainty (Adams, 2019). It is evident in the testimonies of family members born after the abductions took place that the issue is deeply embedded within their lives. In part, they had grown up in a situation where the actions of the paramilitaries impacted not only on the victim but on the whole family unit. Participants explained how the lack of information, and witnessing the distress of their parents caused wider ramifications for their generation, burdening them with a legacy of fear and unresolved grief, and compounding a sense of uncertainty in the world around them. For many, this situation prevails even 40 years on.

> 'It took its toll on me emotionally and I can't imagine what it is doing to direct family members of the deceased, whenever I felt that...It's, it's a heavy cross to bear now, I can only imagine what it's like for them'.

Fear was a constant companion across the generations. Part of the process of control in the aftermath of the violence was to increase fear and threaten anyone who spoke out. For families of disappearances in Sri Lanka, this process was described as psychological warfare to ensure compliance and control (Somasundaram, 2007). This also holds true for Northern Ireland.

FAMILY ACTIVISM

As the political context changed in Northern Ireland, the issue of disappearances gradually emerged into the public arena, primarily due to family activism. In the first instance, this activism was aimed at drawing attention to the occurrence of disappearances, but as the women stood up and spoke out, they realised that it had the effect, for them, of taking back control. This came at great personal cost as the women began to face threats and violence when they went public with their stories. Nonetheless, without their public work, the families are convinced that their loved ones would never have been given the attention that was so desperately needed. Family members reflected on other disappeared cases that they had heard of within the community, but which were never formally reported, and attributed this to the lack of public activism from the respective families.

> 'I've always said… there was a lot of people out there. And, for some reason or other -whether their families are dead, or, they haven't came forward'.

For progress to be made on the recovery of the body of a loved one, the family members had to be very publicly active. For some participants, it took some time to get to this place, but they said that once they met other families they felt compelled to speak out, both for the sake of their loved one, and for the sake of the larger group.

> 'If I don't do this then I am letting down not only myself, I am letting Z down mostly but I am also letting other people, who need that information beside me. I am letting them down. So you want to do what's right. Well do it whether you like it or you don't. You know we all need help'.
> 'I feel that no matter what anybody done to me, I have to speak out and if I don't, I am betraying my brother'.

In highlighting their loved one's cases, a key area of common concern was the need to avoid antagonising the paramilitaries or, by extension, the community around them.

> 'Y (sibling) and myself had a huge difference of opinion... I just thought he was like a bull in a china shop for a few years. He has reined it in now and thankfully X (sibling) with her more emotional, non-political stance, it's become more salient and more important in our narrative than some political point scoring'.

It was clear from interviewing several members of the same family that relationships were, and continue to be, complex. Over time, relationships changed, with some of the younger family members becoming the main lobbyists within the families. Equally, a variety of approaches were often taken by parents. Sometimes, for example, one parent would assume responsibility for highlighting their loved one's case, whilst the other remained silent. For those active, there was a sense, that in lobbying, they had greater control over the situation than those who were silent (Campbell & Demi, 2000).

> 'My mum finds great comfort and it was very beneficial for her to talk about it over the years and to repeat her story and God love her because she did it, that's why we ended up getting Z's body . Daddy took a different approach and he kept quiet. He didn't like to talk about it'.

As reflected in the stories of the participants, there was a clear purpose in, and benefit from, sharing what had happened to them and their families. Achieving a sense of solidarity and sharing one's experiences enabled a reconstruction of a sense of meaning and identity. This is crucial when individuals are living with the complexity and ambiguity of a disappearance (Robins, 2011).

> 'When Mummy became involved with WAVE and they gave her that platform and encouraged her to talk about it, Mum took it like a baton and ran with it, and it was great because she was doing something for Z to try to find him again and because she talked about it so much it was therapeutic for her'.

For the families, the marginalisation experienced within the community was replaced by the solidarity and support of other families experiencing the same traumatic loss.

Affirming and Rehumanising the Dead

For the families, recovery was perceived as a re-emergence of their loved one back into the family unit and back into society more broadly.

'If a person disappears, it's like they never existed'.

Their description of the experience is captured by the idea of *'social ghosts'* in which parents who have lost children continue to have a sense of their presence years after they have died (Stroebe et al., 1992, pp. 1210). The concept of social ghosts was particularly apparent when the families visited the presumed burial sites; many felt that their loved ones were present and waiting to be recovered. Some experienced guilt when they had to leave the site after each search; they felt they were once again letting their relative down and denying them their right to be laid to rest.

Having a loved one disappeared leaves family members in a perpetual state of uncertainty that impedes them in the processing of memories (Eisma & Stroebe, 2021; Jones, 2020). The manner and context in which the disappearance is perpetrated by paramilitaries is strongly tied to this, as the external environment in which the loss occurred contributes to this feeling of emotional and physical disconnection. The participants believed that part of the strategy of republican paramilitaries over the years was to ensure that all traces of their loved ones' existence were removed. Just as the body would fade post-burial, so too would the memories. In this way, the victim would cease to be remembered at a community and societal level.

'He was shot and buried like a dog, they wanted to get rid of him and hoped that it would wither away'.

This concept of withering away not only reflects the decomposition of the body, but the 'enforced forgetting' by those who instigated disappearances (Caicedo & Cardenas, 2018; Garcia-Godos, 2018; Hollander, 2016; Mir, 2020; Robins, 2016).

The secret burial, often followed by the stigmatisation and labelling of the individual in the aftermath of their death, led the families to feel that their loved one's memory had not only been obliterated, but that they had been dehumanised and ceased to matter as human beings. For some of the families, the process of addressing these wrongs began with the first act of speaking out about their loved ones.

> '*It never sunk in when they told us (Z had been recovered), somebody is actually speaking about Z, it was as if he was there, he existed'.*
> '*Z did exist in this world. He was a person; this person did exist, did live and his life was taken from him'.*

For the families, telling the story to others, not only acknowledges the loss, it ensures that it becomes part of public history and reinforces their loved one's existence (Massimi & Baecker, 2011). Rehumanising their loved ones and reaffirming their existence was a key aim of the families. The recovery of a body was the beginning of this reaffirmation, and of a process of reintegrating them back into the family unit.

Transformative Action on the Disappeared.

After years of silence, the first tentative steps towards speaking about the Disappeared, were hugely significant. This process began in 1994 with Margaret McKinney, the mother of Brian McKinney, who disappeared in 1978, visiting some of the other families who had reached out to her after she had highlighted the case publicly. Together the families discovered the commonalities in their cases. This provided a much-needed validation of their suffering given the circumstances of their loss. Reaching out and engaging with other families whose loved ones had disappeared was important as it reduced isolation and bolstered family members in raising the profile of their loved ones. The process was also beneficial because it fostered greater resilience and provided some hope (Adams, 2019).

> '*It's a united voice, it's like a big choir rather than a solo which makes a bigger impact. They (republican paramilitaries) weren't imagining that anything like that would ever happen. They would still say we didn't know anything; we just do whatever we want'.*

For many families, engaging in these acts of defiance was challenging. However, as the families realised that there were many cases of disappearances, they initially sought to raise awareness locally about the issue; this was followed by their coming together at the WAVE Trauma Centre, in 1996, to undertake advocacy as a group. This was an incremental process that focused on building trust between the family members in the disappeared support group, and between the support group and WAVE.

Participants in the study spoke of how, initially, they were all strangers. At first, even engaging with the other families was tentative and met with some concern; individuals worried whether any information would be taken back to PIRA or INLA.

"In terms of all the other families of the Disappeared, at first I was a bit apprehensive – "Who are all these people?" We didn't know one another. You're wary. Did they know all about the IRA involvement and we don't?'

Given the context of the disappearances and the intimacy within communities, participants reflected on how meeting others from outside their community, whilst initially daunting, was ultimately important from the perspective of building trust in others outside their own family. Participants recognised that the group, as a collective force, was the only mechanism available to them if they wanted to highlight their case.

'You know that [group campaigning] is the only avenue that you have. Other than that you have nothing you know. There is no door like 10 Downing Street, there is no door that says IRA, that says all enquiries given. They are not going to give anything. So that's the only avenue you have'.

There were, of course, negative aspects to engaging in advocacy and creating a public profile—many felt that their identity was subsumed by the campaign. They ceased to be an individual and, instead, became known as someone's son or daughter, wife, parent or sibling. This disruption of identity, social roles and relationships (Jakoby, 2012; Lopez-Zeron & Blow, 2015), is often witnessed in the aftermath of a traumatic death, but in the case of the Disappeared, the complexity was intensified (Somasundaram, 2014). In some cases, the connection to the Disappeared became a type of tarnished identity (Bryant et al., 2018), where individuals were labelled and stigmatised and, in some cases, had aspects of their own identity denied.

In undertaking acts of defiance, many of the participants were mindful of the continued power of the paramilitaries. They identified concerns about protecting themselves, given the vulnerability associated with sharing intimate details of their family and the loss they had experienced. They developed strategies for self-protection as they did not want to give any further control to those responsible for their loss by breaking down in interviews or being fully open about how they felt. They did not want to appear any more vulnerable than they felt they were already.

'It was the simple message of "Where are they"?... "Where are our sons, our mother, our father"? ... "give them back to us". That's all we wanted'.

For many of the families, having a support group to rely on mitigated feeling publicly exposed or vulnerable when engaging in public or with the media about the Disappeared (Coulter et al., 2013).

'I'll stand up in front of any of them (republican politicians) and tell them exactly what I want. I'll never tell them how I feel, I'll tell them what I want... I've done it for Z... I've done it for me mum'.

These experiences are common amongst the families of those disappeared across the world (Adams, 2019; Badshah et al., 2021; Danziger & MacLean, 2010; Hollander, 2016; Mir, 2020; Robins, 2016; Smid et al., 2020; Solar, 2021). Given that, in many cases, these families remain within the communities where the disappearances took place, their courage in advocating for their loved ones is all the more remarkable. Some of the journeys made by the families of those disappeared have been public and high profile, such as in the case of the Mothers of the Disappeared de Plaza de Mayo in Argentina who confronted the Junta in the 1980's (Crenzel, 2020). Others have not had the same public profile. For example, young women lobbying for the return of their fathers and brothers in Pakistan have had to take up political roles in order to be heard and to gain traction on their loved ones' cases (Hadid, 2020). Being forced into this public and political role chimes with the experiences of the families of the Disappeared in Northern Ireland.

'It takes the families to publicly state it, as the IRA don't respond otherwise. And this all would have went away, for all of them, if you (WAVE) hadn't been keeping momentum going, to keep it in the public eye'.
'I think that... being involved with WAVE and the other people that had people disappeared, you're carried along in that, so she (Mother) had that hope at the end of the day that she would find him'.

Choosing to speak out, even as the conflict was still ongoing prior to the 1998 Good Friday Peace Agreement, was particularly challenging as the families ran the risk of invoking further violence from the local

Fig. 5.1 Baroness Nuala O'Loan launching the disappeared book detailing who the disappeared were in May 2013 at the Lyric Theatre, Belfast. Photograph ©The Detail

paramilitaries. For many family members, taking these crucial steps forward to break the silence was the only way to keep the connection to their loved one alive and to honour their memory (Fig. 5.1).

FAMILIES UNITED TOGETHER

As the families got to know each other, and as they worked on their own and each other's cases over the years, they formed a tightly knit group that served as the centre point for activism on the Disappeared. The connection between the members became strikingly evident in the position they took on recovery—their unanimous position to this day remains that the issue of the Disappeared will not be addressed until *all* the bodies are recovered. Even as the loved ones of some of the families have been recovered, the group has continued to support and advocate for the families whose loved ones have disappeared. This stance has evolved as the group developed, demonstrating, not only the depth of the relationships but also the impact of this unique experience on the families and their shared understanding of the importance of recovery for all involved.

'I couldn't let it go. I couldn't switch off, I never would have switched off, even yet. I still would like to see them all found, every one of them, because it's only when you go through it, that you realise what every family has gone through and the pain of it and, you know you just can't settle'.

The families believe that it is only those who have gone through similar experiences who can relate to the protracted nature and pain of disappearance. Continuing to fight is, therefore, tied to addressing the unique injustice against the victims and the families and has the ultimate aim of ensuring that the bodies of those disappeared are recovered and that paramilitary control of their narrative is ended. As a result, participants in the study were of the view that they needed to continue to work together to ensure recovery. They articulated a very strong connection to other members of the group.

'We are married into this thing now, you know ... they were there for us so we have to be there for them'.
'Even though we have got Z, I still feel that I want to belong with them'.

As a result of this connection, the families whose loved ones' bodies were recovered have continued to attend events, undertake interviews and highlight the issue. For those waiting for information, the feeling that they have not been abandoned has been reassuring. There is no doubt that, as the circle of those still missing has become smaller, it has become harder for the families who wait; each one worries that they will be the only family not to have their loved one returned.

In some cases in other jurisdictions, group allegiance such as this has been known to have a negative impact on identity and health (Osborne et al., 2009). However, the families of the Disappeared do not believe it has hindered family members from dealing with the grief associated with the loss of their loved one. Such action can be understood as altruism born out of suffering (Vollhardt & Staub, 2011), an empathetic approach that does not hinder individuals who have had similar experiences but can, rather, empower them from a social justice perspective.

'It's not closed yet, and it will not be closed until they are all recovered and all home'.

Whilst each individual experiences this differently and this shifts over time, the group still contends to this day that this strategy is what gives them strength.

Seeing Is Believing.

For the families, the experience of rehumanising the Disappeared is linked to both speaking out and seeking recovery of the remains. However, in addition, the need to bear witness to the physical remains when loved ones' bodies are returned has been viewed by many as essential in getting to a place of resolution. Years of living with the uncertainty, ongoing questions around their existence, their lack of trust and the coercive control at the hands of paramilitaries left the families in a state of disbelief regarding the search and recovery of remains.

> '21 years looking, you weren't prepared to believe anyone or anybody or anything you know'.

For years the family members faced a myriad of misinformation, rumours and lies. Feelings of mistrust permeated all aspects of the families' lives outside their immediate family circle and a small group of close friends. When recovery came it often emerged after weeks of searching and families remained in a state of disbelief until they saw proof that it was their loved one.

> 'I wasn't even convinced that down in (named place) the day he was found... How do we know there is something in that friggin hole?'

This lack of trust dominated the entire recovery process. When recoveries took place families were placed into a protracted waiting period (often up to six weeks) for DNA confirmation of their loved one's identity. Whilst the recovery gave the families hope, it also evoked uncertainty.

> 'I wouldn't have trust fully [in republican paramilitaries] because I would have thought to myself "right they are only saying this to get us to forget about it"'.

The uncertainty regarding identifying the remains was not without foundation. In June 2015, during a search for Joe Lynskey, the ICLVR recovered a body in County Meath. As his family travelled to the site, the team discovered a second body leading them to believe that they had actually found the bodies of Seamus Wright and Kevin McKee, who had also been reportedly secretly buried in that area two months after Joe. The emotional impact of believing that recovery had been achieved only for this hope to be dashed is reflected in an interview given by Maria Lynskey at the time of the search. She indicated that she had believed the whole day that it was her uncle but now had to come to terms with the fact that this might not be the case (McDonald, 2015).

Sinn Fein President Gerry Adams at the time acknowledged how difficult the situation was for the families concerned,

'The uncertainty over who has been recovered must be hugely traumatic for the families involved. I am sure the Commission (ICLVR) will move as speedily as it can to verify the identity of those who have been found' (O'Brien, writing in the Irish Times, 2015).

The confirmation of a positive DNA result represented, not only the end of the uncertainty that began with the disappearance (Fondebrider, 2002), it also ended the feeling that their loved one continued to be at the mercy of those responsible for their death. However, often family members, described how they still wanted to see or touch the remains or the property of their loved one—they needed to know, outside of any process, that it was, in fact, their relative.

However the need for physical proof was often not possible, given the parameters of the ICLVR's remit. One of the challenges for family members was that they were unable to come close to the burial ground. They were always kept at a discrete distance. For some, this caused distress as they wanted to see how their loved ones had been buried. A review of the processes for the recovery of politically motivated disappearances across the world highlights that, in some countries, such as Iraqi Kurdistan and Ethiopia, the families assisted the archaeologists and forensic team with the recovery (Fondebrider, 2002). Whilst this is not possible under the process that exists for the ICLVR, the families' wish for physical proof of recovery is understandable, given the underlying issues around how the secret burial of their loved one was managed by the paramilitaries for decades.

'I'd like to be able to see things and then be able to believe it and deal with it in that way. Some people just don't want to go there, but I'm not like that,

I like to see it, be able to take it in and understand it for myself then, but we weren't allowed to do that'.

As mentioned, a number of family members wanted to see the remains. This was important, not only as *proof* of their loss but also because it had cultural significance. In Ireland, having an open coffin and viewing the remains is an important part of the funeral ritual (Ronan, 2021). Obviously, given the nature of death and burial, an open coffin was not possible for the Disappeared. Families felt this to be a further denial of the right of their loved one to be respected within the normal cultural traditions of the community.

'You know even someone coming home to you in the coffin, like I mean you can't look in the coffin, that's the part that's missing'.

Given the length of time taken to recover the remains, seeing the remains were often valued by the families as one of the final acts of acknowledging the death and recovery of their loved ones. It also allowed them the opportunity to place family pictures and religious medals and symbols in the coffin. Those who were able to see their loved one's remains did not express regret at their choice. Even though the remains were skeletal, as traumatic as that was, bearing witness to the physical remains was important to the families in laying their loved ones to rest.

'I was determined. That kept me going those six weeks we had to wait for confirmation because I thought I definitely have to do this. I'm definitely glad I did it. I couldn't not have done it' .

For some they also needed the feeling of touching their loved ones remains.

'I literally lifted bits and kissed it ... that was a great comfort to me, a great comfort'
   'You know I saw prominent teeth and I knew right away and I said "thanks lads that gives me peace of mind"... it did, it did' .

Whilst the ICLVR has a very strong support structure for families, they do not arrange for the families to see the remains; nor do they provide support during that process, as this is beyond their remit. On each occasion, this is arranged with the undertaker. However, of note are the World

Health Organisation's Guidelines on the Management of Dead Bodies in Disaster Situations (World Health Organisation, 2004) that advocate for allowing the remains of a loved one to be accessed should that be the family's wish.

For many of the participants, seeing the remains was considered important at a psychological level. One of the greatest challenges in coming to terms with a loved one's death is making sense of what has happened (Bath, 2010; Neimeyer et al., 2006). For the families, seeing the remains was confirmation of their loved one's return; it demystified the condition of their body and assisted some family members in bidding farewell to their loved ones. One of the participants recalled how his mother had wanted rosary beads placed in the coffin with her son before he was taken from the secret burial site. In the absence of being able to see him at the site, she wanted something physical to connect her with him; she wanted, as the mothers in Mexico did, to have a connection to her son and, above all, for his religious and cultural needs to be met. The rosary beads were placed in the coffin beside him before he was carried from the site by the ICLVR search team.

'She wanted them (rosary beads) with him because like in spirit she was probably with him all the time but she wanted something physical to say, do you know, at the end of the day it was her son'.

Like the rosary beads, belongings have had a deep significance for the families. Belongings are tangible proof of identity and access to them has given great relief to some families.

'We got Z's necklace back and that meant something. U (sister) had given him the wee chain around his neck… It was part of Z. It's nice to get something that he actually had on his person'.

At times, whilst the families waited for DNA confirmation, for example, the belongings provided reassurance that the body recovered was in fact their loved one.

'During those six weeks I never thought it was not Z, I didn't doubt it because Z had a wee false tooth… and then the chain around his neck'.

In many cases, the manner and type of clandestine burial of the Disappeared preserved the belongings so well that they were easily recognisable to family members. Bogs, where most of those recovered have been buried, are known to preserve bodies, clothing and other artefacts for centuries or even millennia (McClean, 2008, p302). Seamus Heaney described the bogs of Ireland as a *'landscape that remembered everything that happened in it'* (Keefe, 2018).

> *'His jumper and shoes was as good as the first day. The bog kept them you know and maybe him too'.*
> *'I have still got his trainers, I remember them and that coat he was wearing'.*

For the families, belongings were viewed as an extension of a loved one. They represented who they were and the life they had lived (Hallam & Hockey, 2020) (Fig. 5.2).

The testimonies of the participants reflected how, in the early days of the ICLVR's work, family members were given the clothes if they wanted

Fig. 5.2 A little gold cross found under clothing at one of the search sites. Photograph © Family member

them. In later years, however, this process was stopped, although some received coins, or buttons or toggles off duffel coats, for example. There is no doubt that these belongings, where they were available, provided comfort to the families because they were often the only physical connection they had to their loved ones. However, in many cases, it was not possible to release all of the belongings. This could be for a variety of reasons, including health and safety (given the nature of the burial in bog land) and because of the parameters of the ICLVR legislation (Knupfer, 2021). Some of the family members have found this deeply upsetting as they believe that the items belong to the family and should be returned to them.

> *'I would have liked to have had some pieces of his clothes, even if it was totally ragged. They said he had a zip up cardigan. Who gives them the authority to say to us "no you can't have them?" '*
> *'Not having anything belonging to him, even a piece of coat or whatever. You think well that was the last thing he had on, that was the only thing that we can have belonging to him'.*

Resentment has grown where belongings have been held for years, particularly when family members have become seriously ill and want to have them returned to them before they die. The overriding fear is that these deeply personal items will be lost forever and never returned to their rightful place amongst the family.

> *'How can officialdom overrule this and say "no, we can destroy it or we can bury it"'.*

The significance of belongings is reflected across the international literature (Roster, 2001; Hunter, 2008; Richardson, 2014; Tidball-Binz, 2017; Hallam & Hockey, 2020), where it is contended that if there is deritualisation, whereby the death has been denied and it has not been possible to undertake the rituals associated with death and burial, individuals may experience difficulty separating themselves from their loved one's belongings (Guillard, 2017, p. 492).

> *'That's the only thing we have left of our Z. Everybody else, as far as I believe, all got their family members' stuff back, and we are getting robbed of that as well'.*

Respect Restored—Righting the Wrongs of the Past.

Throughout the searches, the relationships between the families and those searching became very important. The search team from the ICLVR always familiarised themselves with the details of who they were searching for, and the family members who were waiting. Mutual respect was at the centre of this relationship.

'They are totally committed to… doing their utmost to get a final end to it'.

When bodies were recovered, it was important for the families that it was the ICVLR search team, with whom they had established a relationship of trust, who would carry their loved ones from the burial sites to waiting hearses. This was seen by the families as affording their loved ones dignity and respect. It was also seen as a supportive gesture to the families by the ICLVR given how traumatic the recovery process was for all present.

'I can still see that today, the Commission (ICLVR) bringing his remains up from the beach, rather than the undertakers. It was lovely'.

'I will always remember it was the people that was doing the digging, Jon and the Guards leading, when they carried it up (coffin from the burial site), but it was tough'.

(Fig. 5.3)Whilst these were small gestures, they were important for the families. Working with the ICLVR team in the years preceding, and in the immediate lead-up to, the search enabled a relationship to be built between the team and the families. During this time the families felt that their experiences were recognised and validated. The families became known to all of the search teams and often a picture was placed close to the site by the family so that the ICLVR team might feel connected to their loved one whilst they worked. This engagement by the search team at a personal level was vital in providing some comfort to the families (Fondebrider, 2002)

Signs of respect were so very welcome by the families. They recall an escort provided by An Garda Siochana to each of the hearses bringing the Disappeared from the mortuary in Dublin to the border with Northern Ireland. Participants recounted how meaningful this was.

Fig. 5.3 Members of ICLVR's forensic search team carry the remains of Peter Wilson from Waterfoot beach- November the 2nd 2010. Photograph ©Mal McCann

> 'The other thing that Daddy was really taken with, which is quite strange, it's simple things, he got a guard of honour from the Gardai down to the border'.
>
>   'I'll never forget that and they says… 'we will take him home' and, God love them, the Guards… they took us and gave us an escort'.

At a community level, there were also signs that respect had returned for the families, as neighbours and members of the community attended the wakes or came to the funerals. The numbers attending were often in sharp contrast to the lack of support or engagement offered over the years. Funerals in Ireland are a somewhat unique affair; individuals are not formally invited but are expected to show up to demonstrate their respect and support for the family. Having tens or hundreds of people attend a funeral would not be unusual. However, the families had no sense of how much support would be forthcoming at their loved ones' funerals. The fact that the wakes and funerals of the Disappeared were so well attended, with visits from right across the community was of great comfort to the families. It was repeatedly reflected in the testimonies of participants how surprised they were at the level of support.

'The two days that he stayed in the house they came out of the woodwork the amount of people. The roads were all closed and we didn't ask anyone to close the roads'.
'I think everyone came out in a kind of solidarity'.

In addition to offering support, the symbolism of the community being present felt like a righting of the wrongs committed against the families. Many of the participants remarked that some in the community expressed embarrassment at how the family had been treated, others, deep regret for the nature of their loss. As well as the ritual around the funeral, the ability to lay their loved one to rest in the local church graveyard meant that the family could feel that their loved one had now been accepted back into the community.

'Giving someone a burial in their local graveyard is a way of showing respect for the person who has died, that they were human, and a part of society. It's important to keep that connection, that they're now part of this society and back with their family'.

This restoration of respect was hugely significant, not only in reinstating the identity and existence of the Disappeared as members of their communities, but also in providing an environment in which respect was returned to their families. The families felt that, for the community, the opportunity to support the family was an attempt to right the wrongs of the past.

References

Adams, J. (2019). Enforced disappearance: Family members experiences human rights review. *Human Rights Review, 20*(3), 335–360.

Badshah, I., Ashraf, S., Faiz, F. & Kamran, M. (2021). *Voices of dissent and the political activism of left behind females of baloch enforced disappeared persons,* Ilkogretim Online. Available at: https://doi.17501/ilkonline2021.04.333 (Accessed: October 12 2021).

Bath, D. (2010). Separation from loved ones in the fear of death. *Death Studies, 34*(5), 404–425.

Bryant, E., Schimke, E., Brehm, N., & Uggen, C. (2018). Techniques of neutralisation and identity work among accused genocide perpetrators. *Social Problems, 65*(4), 584–602.

Caicedo, J. & Cardenas, J. (2018). Rethinking the Colombian transition to peace through the South African experience. In Pabon, F. (Ed.). *Truth, Justice and reconciliation in Colombia transitioning from violence.* Routledge.

Campbell, C. & Demi, A. (2000). Adult children of father's missing in action. An examination of emotional distress, grief and family hardiness. *Family Relations, 49*(3), 267–276.

Coulter, S., Campbell, J., Duffy, J., & Reilly, I. (2013). Enabling social work students to deal with the consequences of political conflict: Engaging with victim/ survivor service users and a pedagogy of discomfort. *Social Work Education, 32*(4), 439–452.

Crenzel, E. (2020). The ghostly presence of the disappeared in Argentina. *Memory Studies, 13*(3), 253–266.

Danziger, N. & MacLean, R. (2010). *Missing lives.* Dewi Lewis Publishing.

Eisma, M., & Stroebe, M. (2021). Motion regulatory strategies in complicated grief: A systematic review. *Behavior Therapy, 52*(1), 234–249.

Fondebrider, L. (2002). Reflections on the scientific documentation of human rights violations. *International Review of the Red Cross, 84*(848), 885–891.

Garcia-Godos, J. (2018). Transitional justice in Peru: Lessons for Colombia. In Pabon, F. (Ed.) *Truth, Justice and reconciliation in Colombia transitioning from violence.* Routledge.

Guillard, V. (2017). Understanding the process of the disposition of a loved one's possession using a theoretical framework of grief. *Consumption Markets & Culture, 20*(5), 477–496.

Hadid, D. (2020). *Young women in Pakistan now lead the fight against secret abductions.* npr.org, 3 July. Available at: https://npr.org/2020/7/13/890 328374/young-women-in-pakistan-now (Accessed: September 14 2020).

Hallam, E., & Hockey, J. (2020). *Death, memory and material culture.* Routledge.

Hollander, T. (2016). Ambiguous loss and complicated grief: Understanding the grief of parents of the disappeared in Northern Uganda. *Journal of Family Theory & Review, 8*(3), 1–28.

Hunter, E. (2008). Beyond death: Inheriting the past and giving to the future, Transmitting the legacy of one's self. *OMEGA-Journal of Death and Dying, 56*(4), 313–329.

Jakoby, N. (2012). Grief as a social emotion: Theoretical perspectives. *Death Studies, 36*(36), 679–711.

Jones, L. (2020). Grief and loss in displaced refugee families. Child, Adolescent and family refugee mental health. In Song, S. & Ventevogel, P. (Eds.). *Child adolescent and family refugee mental health.* Springer.

Keefe, P. (2018). Say nothing. *A true story of murder and memory in Northern Ireland*. Williams Collins.

Knupfer, G. (2021). *Destroying clothing*. Correspondence to WAVE Trauma Centre. (On file with author).

Lopez-Zeron, G., & Blow, A. (2015). The role of relationships and families in healing from trauma XE "trauma." *Journal of Family Therapy, 39*(4), 580–597.

Massimi, M. & Baecker, R. (2011). *Dealing with death in design: Developing systems for the bereaved. Proceedings of the SIGCHI Conference on Human Factors in Computing Systems 1001–1010*, Vancouver, Canada, 07–05–2011–12–05–2011.

McClean, S. (2008). Bodies from the bog: Metamorphosis, non-human agency and the making of collective memory. *Trames, 12*(3), 299–308.

McDonald. H. (2015). *Fresh dig continues after suspected IRA victim's bodies found*. The Guardian. 26 June. Available at: https://www.theguradian.com/world/2015/jun/26/fram-dig-disappeared-suspected-ira-victims-bodies-found (Accessed: June 12 2020).

Mir, R. (2020). Women and violence: A comprehensive study of the socio-economic and political status of half widows in Kashmir. *South East Journal,* 17. Available at: https://www.academia.edu/37435542/Women_and_Violence_A_Comprehensive_Study_on_the_Socio_economic_and_Political_Status_of_Half_widows_in_Kashmir (Accessed: January 9 2021).

Neimeyer, R., Baldwin, S. & Gillies, J. (2006). Maintaining bonds and reconstructing meaning. Mitigating complications in bereavement. *Death Studies, 30*(8), 715–738.

O'Brien, T. (2015). *Bodies of Seamus Wright and Kevin McKee found, The Irish Times,* 27 June. Available at: https://www.irishtimes.com/news/ireland/irish-news/bodies-of-seamus-wright-and-kevin-mckee-believed-found-1.2265431 (Accessed: July 15 2021).

Osborne, K., Baum, F., & Ziersch, A. (2009). Negative consequences of community group participation for women's mental health and wellbeing: Implications for gender aware social capital. *Journal of Community & Applied Social Psychology, 18*(3), 212–224.

Richardson, T. (2014). Spousal bereavement in later life: A material cultural perspective. *Mortality, 19*(1), 61–79.

Robins, S. (2011). Towards victim-centred transitional justice: Understanding the needs of families of the disappeared in post conflict Nepal. *International Journal of Transitional Justice, 5*(1), 75–98.

Robins, S. (2016). Discursive approaches to ambiguous loss: Theorising community based therapy after enforced disappearance. *Journal of Family Theory & Review, 8*(3), 1–32.

Ronan, M. (2021). Funerals in time of Coronavirus. *Irish Journal of Sociology,* *29*(2), 236–240.

Roster, C. (2001). Letting go: The process and meaning of dispossession in the lives of consumer. *Advances in Consumer Research, 28,* 425–430.

Salih, M., & Samarasinghe, G. (2017). Families of the missing in Sri Lanka: Psychosocial considerations in transitional justice mechanisms. *The Missing: International Review of the Red Cross, 99*(2), 497–517.

Smid, G., Blaauw, M., & Lenferink, L. (2020). Relatives of enforced disappeared persons in mexico: Identifying mental health and psychosocial support needs and exploring barriers to care intervention. *Journal of Mental Health and Psychosocial Support in Conflict Affected Areas, 18*(2), 139–149.

Solar, C. (2021). Forced disappearances and the inequalities of a global crime. *Alternatives: Global, Local and Political, 46*(1), 17–22.

Somasundaram, D. (2007). Collective trauma XE "trauma" in northern Sri Lanka: A qualitative psychosocial-ecological study. *International Journal of Mental Health Systems, 1*(5), 1–27.

Somasundaram, D. (2014). *Scarred communities.* Psychosocial impact of man-made and natural disasters on Sri Lankan society.

Stroebe, M., Gergen, K., Gergen, M., & Stroebe, W. (1992). Broken hearts or broken bonds: Love and death in historical perspective. *American Psychologist, 47*(10), 1205–1211.

Tidball- Binz, M. (2017). Using forensic science to care for the dead and search for the missing: in conversation with Dr Morris Tidball- Binz. *International Red Cross Humanitarian Debate: Law, policy, action. The Missing, 99*(905), 689–707.

Vollhardt, J., & Staub, E. (2011). Inclusive altruism born of suffering: The relationship between adversity and prosocial attitudes and behavior towards disadvantaged outgroups. *American Journal of Orthopsychiatry, 81*(3), 307–315.

World Health Organisation (2004) *Guidelines on the management of dead bodies in disaster situations.* W.H.O.

CHAPTER 6

Political Support, Justice and Taking Back Control

Abstract Whilst the experience of the families of the Disappeared involved a very painful personal journey, there was also a very public element to this process. Events at a local, national and international level impacted the experience of the families, and these socio-political events often guided the process that was possible. Central to these events were the emergence of a ceasefire by paramilitary groups, the ongoing peace process negotiations and the involvement of international political figures. The involvement of President Clinton was highlighted as particularly significant for the families. Alongside this political engagement, the role of local communities in coming to support families and acknowledging the use of disappearances was a significant issue for the families. This chapter explores the impact of these events and tracks how the personal experiences of families was very much impacted by ongoing external events.

Keywords Activism · Politics · Disappearance · Awakening · International involvement · Clinton

LOCAL AND INTERNATIONAL BROKERAGE

As the families started to become more proactive in highlighting the deaths of their loved ones, a number of external factors facilitated the process. One central driver was the move by republican and loyalist paramilitaries towards engaging in a Peace Process in the 1990s. This started with the PIRA ceasefire on August 31, 1994, with the INLA ceasefire following on August 22, 1998.

> 'They (the British and Irish Governments) couldn't set up the commission (ICLVR) without the cooperation of Sinn Fein who had turned their guns into chairs at that stage, so it couldn't have been done without Sinn Fein being involved, which is pretty evident'.

Whilst, for the families, the ceasefires were welcome, they did not remove the fear and underlying sense of threat that existed for them within their community. Neither did they remove the feeling of being controlled that still existed for the families. The families knew that, without cooperation from PIRA and INLA, information on the Disappeared would not be forthcoming. As the families started to raise public awareness about the Disappeared, paramilitary shootings, assaults and bombings continued, albeit at a reduced level, and this was enough to ensure that fear and a sense of threat were omnipresent for them (Hogg & Butler, 2018). It was 2005 before PIRA 'officially stood down' to enable the democratic process to progress under the leadership of Sinn Fein (Tonge, 2014) and, by this point, the violence was significantly reduced. However, cooperation on information sharing was still reliant on Sinn Fein and the IRSP engaging where necessary.

In their testimonies, it is evident that the participants largely believed that, in coming to a political agreement, republican paramilitaries were forced, through a series of external brokerage processes to engage on the issue of the Disappeared. This engagement then meant that the issue of the Disappeared was opened up to national and international scrutiny. This was vital, as the paramilitaries' key strategy up to this point had been to keep the issue of disappearances localised and hidden.

> 'Well with WAVE and the media and politicians and all now behind it, it, it has taken it all to the surface, and it's a lot harder to hide from it and with the political situation the way it is at the minute everyone has to clean their hands, and the sooner they clean them all the better'.

According to the families, bringing the issue into the public realm at a local, national and international level was crucial in ultimately bringing about the recovery of the bodies of the Disappeared. Their testimonies reflect that the external brokerage, particularly by the US Administration, was the turning point in enabling the recovery of their loved ones.

> *'They (Sinn Fein and the IRSP) didn't do it for our reasons, they done it for their own reasons really, didn't they, they wanted something in return, didn't they. And they must have wanted something bigger'.*

Political brokerage, precipitated by the rising voices of the family members brought the issue of the Disappeared to the fore. Ultimately, the Disappeared became an issue in the negotiations between the British, Irish and US Administrations, Sinn Fein and the IRSP. Whilst political will was essential, it was noted by the families that the Good Friday Agreement provided a necessary framework for Sinn Fein and the IRSP to support the creation of the ICLVR which was ultimately the solution needed by the families.

> *'This wouldn't have been done without the Commission, without the Good Friday Agreement, without being able to offer immunity and confidentiality and all that goes with that'.*

The ICLVR gave the parties the means by which to address enforced disappearances, by shifting the focus away from prosecutions and account-ability towards the recovery of the bodies. For the families, the ICLVR gave them hope that they could finally lay their loved ones to rest.

POLITICAL ENGAGEMENT

Whilst the involvement of the US Administration and the British and Irish Governments was central to achieving the legislation to enable the creation of the ICLVR, the families of the Disappeared had long been lobbying at a local level. The families began a series of engagements with a variety of political leaders after the story of the Disappeared first broke in 1994. Before the support group formed, some family members had started to engage in meetings with senior local and national politicians; this served to slowly raise the political profile of the Disappeared. Whilst these meetings were perceived as useful and a certain amount of pressure may have been levied, participants in the study were of the view that they did not bring the change needed to force republican paramilitaries to reveal where the bodies of the Disappeared were located. Whilst the families hoped that a moral argument for the recovery of the Disappeared would be enough to bring change, this was not the case.

> *'We had years of her speaking to John Major, Mo Mowlam and countless politicians and everything but these people don't have an influence on the IRA'.*

The US Administration had been actively engaged in early work on the Peace Process, but this had intensified during the 1990s. Despite the local-level lobbying, the real breakthrough came when Margaret McKinney met the Clintons in Washington in May 1998. This meeting came about because Sandra Peake the current CEO of WAVE wrote to the First Lady, Hillary Rodham Clinton, asking for a meeting. WAVE had secured funding from the special support programme (Peace 1 funding) to enable some victims and family members to attend a trauma education course hosted by the Peace Building Institute at the Eastern Mennonite University in Harrisburg Virginia,[1] and it was hoped that a meeting with the Clintons could be arranged during this trip.

> *'Who was going to break them at the end of the day it was President Clinton probably the most powerful man in the world. Probably threatening them with your Sinn Fein money drying up here, if you don't do something about those disappeared people'.*

For families to have access to the most powerful leader in the world, and to gain a direct commitment that he would help broker the return

---

[1] The first PEACE Programme (PEACE I), known as the Special Support Programme for Peace and Reconciliation in Northern Ireland, was agreed by the European Commission on December 7, 1994. The aim of the Programme was to show the European Union's solidarity with the people of Northern Ireland and the border counties of Ireland in their search for peace and reconciliation. It was created as a partnership between the European Commission, the governments of Ireland and the United Kingdom, and was based on the findings of a European Commission Taskforce set up to look at ways of giving practical assistance to the people of Northern Ireland and the border counties of Ireland.

of Margaret's son and the other Disappeared victims was a seismic development. Not only did the legacy of this meeting feature strongly for the families, but 15 years after he met Margaret, President Bill Clinton—recounting that meeting in a TV documentary—revealed how it had also made an indelible impression on his own memory.

'She was a very impressive woman just in her simple love for her son. She was willing to go on with her life but she wanted her baby back so she could bury him properly' (.*President Clinton, 'The Disappeared' film* (Millar, 2013)

International involvement at such a crucial juncture was a game changer for the families in their fight for the return of their loved ones' bodies. However, they were very much aware that this brokerage only had traction because *'the time was right'*. The Good Friday Peace Agreement had been signed one month prior to Margaret McKinney's meeting with President Clinton in the White House. All of this combined to bring about the change that was needed.

'It was probably through a combination, of the fact that it was the right thing to do, but politically it would help them (Sinn Fein and IRSP). It had to be solved or they wouldn't benefit from American support. And over history that is usually the case or it (the disappeared) might not have come to the fore'.

The overriding sense of the participants is that the issue of the Disappeared was addressed only because there was a wider benefit, particularly for Sinn Fein. They believe that it was the relationship between Sinn Fein and the US Administration that enabled the brokerage undertaken by President Clinton to bring a solution to the plight of the Disappeared families.

'If there was nothing in it for them (Sinn Fein), they would never have admitted this here only for this. Remember they were getting visas to visit the States where they were barred for decades. Gerry Adams and all and then the States was opening up to them and they liked what they seen and dollars flowing in and they most likely said this is what we have to do to continue here'.

The families were adamant that the relationship the Americans had with Sinn Fein was the key factor in their success. This was not just due to President Clinton's role in the process, but also to the involvement of successive US Administrations in Northern Irish affairs. The credibility they had amongst the community, including the paramilitaries was a powerful force for change. It has been argued that it was US involvement over many years that helped to bring about the PIRA ceasefire in August 1994 (O'Dowd, 2010). The families believed that, concerned about their reputation, Sinn Fein had embarked on a process of damage limitation by now engaging on the issue of the Disappeared.

'What they did - disappearing these people - it came back to haunt them'.

The families were of the view, that as Sinn Fein gained increased international recognition, they had to manage their legacy and the potential impact of the issue of disappearances on international audiences. In claiming responsibility for some of the disappearances, Sinn Fein, sought to manage any fall out that would arise in relation to their failing to help recover the bodies. When family members travelled to the USA from 2004 to 2006 they felt that there was a negative reception from some political quarters; they believed that this was a result of the perception that they were challenging Sinn Fein in a political capacity.

'When P (another family member) and I went to America for the first time to meet with members of Congress and others with an interest in Ireland, one of them got on the phone to someone in Belfast ... and whoever it was on the phone said: "tell them to get back to Belfast. We said give us 30 minutes"'.

However, the families were of the view that, when it became clear that their focus was solely on humanitarian recovery, rather than political lobbying in the USA, the reception they received was more positive.

1999 PUBLIC ACKNOWLEDGEMENT

It was on the back of this international brokerage some 10 months later, in March 1999, that PIRA—followed by INLA at a later stage—released the list of the Disappeared. However, as mentioned, the families believed this list to be incomplete. The public significance of this is captured in a BBC News headline on June 7, 1999, which states that the Disappeared had returned *'to haunt Ireland's conscience'.* (BBC News headline, 1999a) For the families, the inclusion of their loved one's name was both significant and traumatic.

'There was a sense of me feeling a bit guilty but there was a sense of shock, and a sense of, a wee bit of a sense of relief that it's out in the open'.

For the families, seeing a list that included their loved one's names evoked feelings of shock and guilt, as well as relief that they finally had official confirmation that their loved one was dead. It ended the uncertainty, but also the hope that their loved one might still be alive. The relief that the cases were now public was also tinged with apprehension regarding how the community would react. Some families were fearful that this official recognition would lead to their further marginalisation. The testimonies of the participants in the study also reflect the immense concern they still had regarding the influence the paramilitaries continued to have over the community and how this might shape how the issue was perceived at a community level (Hogg & Butler, 2018).

Notwithstanding this ongoing fear, many participants spoke of how this was a positive time as they could now bring the issue of the disappearances out into the open; this enabled them to start talking about their loved ones and the circumstances of their disappearance. This had a significant impact on community dynamics. It also started a process of reversing the isolating and stigmatising effect of the disappearances. It was, too, a relief to see public acknowledgement of the culpability of the paramilitaries, and recognition of the duplicitous tactics—lies, deceit and denial—they had used to keep the families in the dark for over two decades.

'At the time I said to myself... all the lies that was told from '72 to '99... this was the first time they had told the truth, maybe they were telling the truth where my Z was buried, because they gave Z's whereabouts'.

However, with the public acknowledgement, also came the paramilitaries' efforts at justifying the disappearances. The paramilitaries doubled down on labelling the Disappeared as 'informers', or people who had engaged in antisocial behaviour that was detrimental to the republican cause. In other words, there were significant efforts made to suggest that the Disappeared had brought about their own demise.

'Informers were a huge thing at that time. They (families) would have been isolated, polarised, no doubt in saying they would have been targeted afterwards'.

For some families, there was also the disappointment of their loved one not being named on the 1999 PIRA list. There was a dichotomy between, on the one hand, wanting your loved one listed as a form of acknowledgement, whilst recognising that inclusion on this list represented confirmation that your loved one had, indeed, been killed and secretly buried.

> 'We were hoping which is a strange thing to do, that your father's name is on more or less an execution list'.

For those families who believed that their loved one was dead and should have been on the list, it represented a further injustice and a feeling that the family would get left behind as their case remained unconfirmed, unacknowledged and therefore, unaccounted for.

> 'It was a right slap in the mouth that, I couldn't believe that, I took that very bad. I knew in my heart he was, he was dead and I knew they were the cause of it, and the cover up, so then why go and put other names in and not... his'.

However, despite some not being on the list, work on their respective cases did continue leading ultimately to their loved ones being recovered. The impact of the 1999 PIRA and INLA statements also heralded a change at a community and political level. For some time, the families continued to feel a sense of shock around the sudden publication of the list—they had had no prior warning of any process, or that any statement was imminent, until the day before its release when some received a visit from republican representatives.

> 'He read out this statement from Oglaigh na hEireann , you know it was a prepared statement. He stood on the fuckin doorstep and read it (statement from the IRA)'.

The emotions associated with this experience cannot be underestimated; many family members were left with the task of telling their parent(s) or siblings or children that their loved one had now been confirmed as dead (Fig. 6.1).

Fig. 6.1   The funeral of Peter Wilson 37 years after he disappeared in 1973. Photograph © Brendan Murphy

Political Framing and Religious Engagement

All of the families of the Disappeared are Catholic and, therefore, looked to the Catholic Church for help at the time of their loved one's disappearance, and in the years afterwards. Whilst there were some exceptions, with individual priests supporting the family and pushing for information, in the main, the families contend that the Church distanced itself from their plight.

> *'The church wanted nothing to do with us'.*

It was felt, therefore, that religious support was politically influenced, and the families felt that they were further isolated and marginalised by the Church during a deeply traumatic period. One family member recalled his experience,

> *'The church didn't want anything to do with us; it was found out… from some of the social worker's documentation… they went to the priest, the local*

parish priest, and he didn't want nothing to do with it. He said he didn't know what he could do for us. This was coming up to Christmas time... no Z... no food in the house - and the local priest didn't know what he could do for us? To me, the Catholic Church should be ashamed of themselves for what they done'.

This left a dark legacy for the families; some believed that the Church, in its neglect, was complicit in the silence that was orchestrated around the families. In not standing up for them, the families believe that the Church, in effect, colluded in their marginalisation. One participant in the study recalled how even when asked directly to support family members, help from the Church was scarce,

'I remember a priest coming and I had got dressed and tidied up and he said 'you don't look too worried'. They didn't help'.

This participant was deeply hurt by the fact that the priest would not help and made no effort to reach out after this meeting, or in the intervening years as she searched for her son. A common finding from the interviews was that no one from the Church proactively offered practical help despite the families attending Mass and contributing to the running and upkeep of their local church. This proved challenging for the families as many had a strong faith and had long looked to the church for support, reassurance and guidance,

'Faith is really important for her, but as I said, back then you hadn't a priest to talk to. It was not a conversation you were encouraged to have or you were afraid to have either, not knowing what could happen'.

Some of the families believe that, over the years, the attitude and stance of the Church did not change, and that the clergy failed to fully understand the impact of the disappearances on the families involved. Even when other deaths in the family took place, the priest would not mention the Disappeared by name, nor the circumstances of their loss at the funeral. This sent a wider message to the community that the fate of their loved one was not even recognised by the Church; this was seen by the families as further justifying the actions of the paramilitaries as they silenced the families and the community.

'Even on me Mum's and me Dad's funeral, Z's name was never mentioned. Especially, at me Mum's funeral, because that picture (of her son Z) *that had the pride of joy you know the pride of place in that kitchen, that was took to the church that day for her funeral. And even that day he never even mentioned Z, which he should have done'.*

Some of the families believe that there was a hierarchy in relation to how Troubles related issues were treated by the Catholic Church. On the one hand, the Church was reluctant to get involved in highlighting the issue of the Disappeared but, on the other, it was commonplace to include republican prisoners and their families in weekly prayers. This approach gives a clear sense that Northern Ireland's conflict was not, in itself, a barrier to receiving religious assistance, but that the issue of the Disappeared was politically framed within the Catholic Church which deemed it best avoided. The families still wonder, if the Church had not been silent, could the campaign of disappearance orchestrated by republican paramilitaries have been stopped sooner; could the Church have played a more active role in recovering the bodies of those disappeared, and spared the families decades of psychological torture; could the families' emotional suffering and isolation have been eased with support from the Church and why was there such a reluctance, on the part of the Church, to help the families?

As in all communities, the Church is a microcosm of wider society and, in some cases, the families believe that some of the priests were sympathetic to the republican movement, and tacitly accepted that the disappearances were justified. If that was the case, they believe that the orchestrated nature of the action taken by the paramilitaries against the families may have had tacit approval too. One participant in the study recounts how a priest engaged with the family when it was confirmed that his brother had been murdered and secretly buried. He believed that the priest was trying to manage any negative views about the PIRA or Sinn Fein that the family may have had.

'At this stage my goat was getting up in a big way, cause your natural reaction is 'they fucking murdered my brother' and me mother is in a bad way and he [priest] is trying to, I could sense that all the talk was that he was like an apologist for the IRA'.

'How dare you come and be an apologist you know what I mean a priest'.

Fig. 6.2 The search site for Charlie Armstrong. A harrowing place of remembrance. Photograph © Cathal McNaughton

This demonstrates the challenges that arise when there is a political framing of the victims. In this case, the participants felt that the priest failed in his pastoral responsibility to the family. However, despite the reluctance of the church to engage with the families, many remained respectful and loyal to the institution. The individual support shown by a small number of priests who stood by the families over the years was a very important source of support (Fig. 6.2).

SYSTEMIC FAILURES

In the case of Northern Ireland, there were infinite examples of systemic failures, whereby the disappearances were not addressed at an institutional level.

'We didn't really know how to handle it (disappearance) because we did not have any support, only ourselves… Nobody in the police or the Guards [sic], or community or anyone else external would have come forward to talk about this and I think that was part of the whole thing'.

In some cases, families were repeatedly failed by a range of institutions and frontline services, such as the police services (north and south); social services; political representatives; and other State institutions. A central difficulty for the families was that their stories of witnessing an abduction, or their assertions that their loved one must have been abducted, were not taken seriously. Amongst the many difficulties the disappearances caused, the absence of a body caused significant issues because without the remains, the families were not able to register their loved ones' deaths, leaving the families in legal and financial limbo (Cronin-Furman & Krystalli, 2020). In 2009, the Northern Ireland Legislative Assembly introduced the Presumption of Death Act (Northern Ireland) 2009. This legislation allowed for deaths to be registered if a loved one was missing for more than seven years. Despite supporting the legislation, the families of the Disappeared did not apply for death certificates. They feared that, by doing so, they would allow the republican movement to avoid returning their loved ones' remains and that they would be betraying their loved ones by not fighting for their return. This was always their priority. This resonates with the experiences of the family members of the Disappeared in Colombia who viewed their Government's decision to issue death certificates in the absence of a body as an attempt to avoid truth and justice (Cronin-Furman & Krystalli, 2020). Whilst the Presumption of Death Act benefitted anyone whose loved one had been missing for more than seven years, it did not adequately address the issue of the Disappeared because of both the issue of accountability and the inherent human rights violations that the families needed acknowledged.

In recent times, records released demonstrate that key institutions were aware that disappearances took place but failed to act.

'Through the records they had at the time, they knew fine rightly that our Z was taken away by the IRA'.

Learning that information was known but not acted upon has led to a further sense of betrayal. In the absence of any police investigation, and in the face of the silence emanating from institutions that should have offered support, the families were forced to assume the role of investigators, often retracing the steps of their loved ones and trying to engage with paramilitaries, either directly or indirectly, to gather information (Baines, 2017; Cronin-Furman & Krystalli, 2020; Edkins, 2019). The families speak of how very little exists in the respective files of either the RUC or An Garda Siochana regarding the abductions. And even the little information that was uncovered by police was not shared with the families, in some cases for over two decades. In one instance, gunpowder residue was found in the car of one of the Disappeared—had this fact been shared with the family it would have ended the years of ambiguity regarding the fate of their loved one. The family also pointed out that it would have confirmed that it was likely a paramilitary-related abduction.

In the absence of any robust investigative police processes, families, desperate for information, arranged meetings through intermediaries with members of the PIRA or INLA. These were frightening experiences, sometimes leading to threats of violence against family members and mostly resulting in misleading information or blanket denials. One participant spoke of her husband's experience of trying to get information from the PIRA when he went to meet them about their son,

> *'He told me it was one of the scariest things he had to do because they were all masked. He was on his own in work clothes, they strip searched him, he had to go into a barn and they talked behind barrels and he didn't see them'.*

The PIRA denied having anything to do with the disappearance of her son and the encounter did not progress the case. Other families received visits from members of the PIRA. One family member recalls how they were promised information regarding her brother's disappearance which was never forthcoming,

> *'They were the people that I asked 'was he tortured' and they says "no" and then I sort of lost it a wee bit and I says to the girl, I said "sure you are sitting there telling lies", I says, I just didn't believe her, you know I just lost trust in the whole lot of them, they weren't people that you could sit and listen to and believe'.*

The experience of the conflicts in Colombia, Sri Lanka and Peru (Haugaard & Nicholls, 2010; Isaacs, 2010; Weliamuna, 2012; Heeke et al., 2015; Sivayokan, 2014; Dewhirst & Kapur, 2015; Dulitizky, 2019a;

Cronin-Furman & Krystalli, 2020; Mir, 2020) similarly highlight systemic failures at a political, governmental, societal and community level which allowed the issue of disappearances in each situation to remain hidden and unaddressed.

Notions of Justice

Justice is a very abstract concept for the families of the Disappeared, and it is something that evolved as time passed by. Traditional notions of justice, whereby the State takes responsibility for investigating and prosecuting crime were never the reality for the families. In fact, justice was something that was almost never considered attainable. There was a widespread belief amongst the families that they had been failed by State authorities, with no meaningful police investigations and no one held to account. This is not peculiar to the issue of the Disappeared but was an ongoing issue during the Troubles. Internationally this has also been commonplace for disappearances in other territories (Gayer & Kiermani, 2020); Lewandowsky et al., 2013; Trajkova, 2019; ; . There were many reasons for the criminal justice system failures, one being that there were multiple jurisdictions involved—the victims were abducted in the north of Ireland but they were then taken to the Republic of Ireland where they were killed and secretly buried. However, on the whole, both police services, the RUC in Northern Ireland and the Garda Siochana in the Republic of Ireland, failed to take responsibility for investigating the cases. This was repeatedly reflected upon by participants in the study as a key failing in the whole response to the disappearances. There was no procedural justice for the Disappeared and the families.

> 'You took the life of someone else and you should be paying the price with life imprisonment - and that's my honest opinion'.

For the families, the ICLVR represented the best opportunity for achieving some form of justice. Whilst the families were not consulted on the remit of the ICLVR, it was accepted as the only means of recovering the bodies, however, the families had to accede that all information provided to the ICLVR would be protected; this was not an insignificant issue for the families. As mentioned earlier, the terms of reference of the ICVLR relate only to the recovery of the bodies of the Disappeared, not to evidence gathering for the purposes of an investigation and future prosecutions. Acceptance of the remit of the ICVLR meant that the families were seriously limiting the possibility of ever achieving the prosecution of those responsible for the murders of their loved ones. Left with little real choice, the families all agree, however, that the return of their loved ones' bodies was of paramount importance.

> 'We got Z's remains back; we had to waive justice, so that's the way it is- you have to accept that'.
>
> 'We got him back, we got him back, I didn't agree with them getting away with murder but then again, it was just like a catch 22. I mean she (Mum) had to get him back so this is the only way to get him'.

However, for some family members, after the harrowing experience of the past 40 years, getting the remains back did, in fact, represent their own personal sense of justice.

> 'In terms of justice people don't know what it's like to not have the bodies back of their loved ones, they don't understand that justice isn't about… court dates and seeing someone go down for it'.
>
> 'It's more important to get your loved one home than to get justice'.

Whilst most of the participants understood that the ICVLR legislation was framed to facilitate the recovery of the bodies rather than accessing justice, they felt that they had been let down by the authorities throughout the duration of their loved one's disappearance.

Throughout their journey, they had to engage in repeated trade-offs to ultimately recover their loved ones' bodies. The fact that they were still at the mercy of the paramilitaries, and that the paramilitaries were then able to gain political currency from the process of recovery, was difficult for the families. Faced with criticism regarding the Disappeared, Gerry Adams (2013) wrote,

> 'As a Republican Leader I have never shirked my responsibility on this issue… The failure thus far to find the remaining bodies is not due to any lack of resolve or cooperation by me or other republicans'.

Statements such as this are important. However, for the participants, those within republican armed groups were not only responsible for the disappearances but also responsible for perpetuating and controlling a continuous campaign of enforced silence against their families and anyone within the community seen to be sympathetic to them. The disappearance was not an isolated incident, rather, a continuous experience of pain and distress. This lifetime of psychological torture inflicted upon the families of the Disappeared was never recognised in any of the statements from republican leaders/representatives and this is seen by the families as a further injustice. One participant shared the view that, at a community level, the perceived transition of republicans from combatants to political activists focused on restorative and peace-building practices. However, it was the victims and their families who were left behind in this metamorphosis.

> *'You know they wanted the world to know that they were the revolutionaries, but now they were the peace people now and they wanted peace and they want to love everybody.. It was going to work for them ones, but it was never going to work for us and the rest of the people'.*

The fact that not all of the bodies have been returned, nor other cases of the Disappeared publicly claimed by republican paramilitaries, reinforces the families' belief that the tactic of denial is still in operation and that information is still being willfully withheld by those responsible and only released when it is strategically useful. This makes it very difficult for the families to talk about justice in any meaningful way. A sense of acceptance and compromise, rather than justice captures their experiences.

> *'At some point it has to end. You can't keep making people pay your whole life'.*

Natural Justice

As a result of their experiences, the families speak about justice specifically as it applies to them. They refer to the needs of the families, and how actions to meet these needs would go some way to quieting the pain they feel. This idea of natural justice emerged in their accounts.

> *'What would make a difference in the whole for the other families is that they will find the rest of them [the bodies], that those responsible will disclose their whereabouts, give the bodies back, give an apology, own up to them and give some comfort to these people'.*

The concept of natural justice does not preclude holding people to account for their actions. However, across both local and international literature the evidence suggests that holding paramilitary or insurgent groups to account for disappearances has proved to be challenging, at best, and, in many cases, impossible as evidenced in Chile (Aguilar & Kovras, 2019), Guatemala (Isaacs, 2010), Sri Lanka (Sivayokan, 2014), Colombia (Haugaard & Nicholls, 2010) and Peru (Dulitizky, 2019a). The barriers to, and the longevity of, the families' quests to bring their loved ones' cases to the fore meant that a reality set in, and attention inevitably moved from retributive justice to recovery justice.

'That's the most important thing, getting them back'.

However, the process and reality of getting loved ones back also confirmed to the families the cruelty of the murder and the clandestine burial. The relief of recovery brought with it other issues.

'They were war crimes that we didn't believe happened. You know who would ever think of taking someone and just putting them in a bog and walking away. That's barbaric'.

The sheer injustice of the entire experience is something the families may never come to terms with.

'It's always been there, that's always been in my head - if I committed a murder 40 years ago and came out and said to the police "I killed someone 40 years ago... this is where they are buried", I would get life imprisonment - why do they not?'

The likely immunity from punishment as a trade-off for information on what happened to the Disappeared was felt as a type of unconscionable abandonment (Cronin-Furman & Krystalli, 2020). The participants in the study recounted how they had felt abandoned throughout the years at a community and societal level, and this feeling of abandonment has been reinforced by their belief that the disappearances were minimised because, politically, they were subsumed into the wider Peace Process. The lack of a comprehensive process for investigating murders under-taken during the Northern Ireland conflict; the reduction of conflict related murder sentences to two years (a condition of the Good Friday

Agreement) (McKittrick & McVea, 2012); and the protection offered through the ICVLR legislation, all contributed to this view. The trade-off, seen as favouring paramilitary groups was felt as an affront to the experience of the families. This sense of victims' needs and rights being sacrificed for the *greater good* is not unique to the Troubles. For example in Macedonia (Volchevska & Zdravkova, 2020); Peru (Garcia-Godos, 2018); Northern Uganda (Hollander, 2016); Mozambique (Zartman & Kremenyuk, 2005); Somalia (Keating & Waldman, 2018); East Timor (Thakur, 2016); Sri Lanka (Jayasundara-Smits, 2018) and Colombia (Caicedo & Cardenas, 2018) the sacrifices expected of the victims have weighed heavily. For the participants in this study, there was a clear sense that their justice was traded as part of the Peace Process and they were the collateral damage.

'Like the Ministers (Government Ministers) in England, would they swallow it, if it had been their loved ones…and still negotiate with these people? No, I don't think so- that definitely wouldn't have happened'.

Ultimately, the families of the Disappeared wanted the option of a retributive justice process, but they felt they had to sacrifice that to secure the recovery of their loved one's bodies. However, despite the focus on recovery, the sense of an absence of justice does not, in practice, diminish for families. Notwithstanding this, several of the participants believe that, regardless of a desire for justice, seeking it is futile. One contends that if you start searching for answers *'It will eat you up'*.

'If you go down that road looking for, for answers, you're never going to get the right answer. And that means you're going to be searching and searching and searching again and with no closure at the end of it'.

He suggests that in searching for answers as a form of justice, you may never achieve the truth given the political context of the deaths. On one level, truth telling can provide a sense of justice for victims and survivors; it can reduce anger, mitigate against vengeance and may help to heal psychological trauma (Mendeloff, 2009). It may also help foster social reconciliation. However, truth telling can also increase the risk of traumatisation (Hamber, 1998) and impede social reconciliation (Isaacs, 2010). There are reports that those who have coped least well with the ambiguous loss of a disappearance have been those who are fixated on truth, seeking closure and focusing on justice (Robins, 2016). Human rights processes that emphasise truth over other aspects of the loss can have a significant impact on the physical and psychological responses of families; this can lead to negative coping. The participant quoted above is of the view that the end will never be in sight if the families hope to achieve answers and redress for their loss.

In the particular case of Northern Ireland, the group solidarity of *fighting as one*, had a significant positive impact on the families' ability to accept the ICVLR processes. Whilst some of the families wanted to progress along a retributive justice route, they ultimately chose not to as they felt it would have affected the families' campaign for recovery.

> *'Some families move on and want to see prosecutions, but I think that would be a wrong move because it would be jeopardising the others who haven't been found. I don't think that my Mum would want that, she believes Z is at rest now'.*

Whilst there was a strong focus within the Families of the Disappeared group on not jeopardising the prospects of those who continued to search for their loved ones. There was also a wider appreciation that finding out information about what happened to a loved one could also be damaging on a psychological level.

> *'I don't know if I could ever do it because one, would they ever tell you the truth and what are you going to gain? I am sure his last moments of being walked down a path and to know he wasn't coming back out of that. Do you want to hear that he said a prayer? Do you want to hear that he begged for his life? I don't know. Things like that aren't good things to hear'.*

The families were acutely aware that victims' responses to truth telling' are individualistic and reflect personal choice (Mendeloff, 2009) and, equally, that such a process can do more harm than good. All the families had questions but were mindful that getting answers to these questions might be more damaging in the longer term. The families were in an invidious position.

> *'I would like to know and I wouldn't like to know at the same time'.*

The families spoke about intrusive images, where they imagined and visualised their loved one's death, however, they also realised that access to the truth might be difficult, given the harsh reality of how their loved one likely died (Testoni et al., 2020).

'Now he's found, he's buried and now it's just that last bit of information, why? And an apology, then I'll die happy. Until that's done, no, it's not closed'.

For many of the families, they still seek an acknowledgement of the harm done to their loved ones and to them. Often, this is expressed as the desire for an apology for the wrong committed. The families have clearly called out what this apology should include: an acknowledgement of innocence; a confirmation that it was a wrongful death; a recognition of the injustice; a recognition of the inhumanity associated with the clandestine burial; and cognisance of the torturous punishment disappearances are for the family unit.

'I'd like them to come out and say that Z was an innocent victim of it all. I don't know why they did it'.

Whilst this request would meet many of the needs of the families, given the repeated denials and mistruths told by the paramilitary groups responsible, they are now sceptical that any meaningful apology, acknowledgement or explanation will ever be forthcoming. A further step often mentioned is that of forgiveness, a highly personal decision that means many things and serves many purposes for the families. Linked to forgiveness is the acknowledgement of the actions of others. The families have spoken about their desire to acknowledge those who helped them over the years; they have even thanked those who came forward with information leading to their loved ones' recovery, fully aware that this could be the perpetrators themselves. This acknowledgement was important for them as a reparative gesture and, for some, it represented a form of forgiveness; a forgiveness that could free them from the bitterness and hatred they had experienced throughout the years.

'I was lucky enough I was able to forgive these people; I'll never forget what they've done, and people look at me sometimes when I say, "I forgive them", but it was wrecking me'.

At a personal level, forgiveness allows family members to escape the negative emotions associated with their loss. However, it is not an all-encompassing forgiveness. One participant described feeling that he could forgive those who killed his brother but could not forgive them for hiding his remains and punishing the family for decades—such was the trauma of the ambiguous loss.

> 'You know it might be a bit of a contradiction to some people... you can forgive somebody for killing your brother, but you can't forgive them for not telling you?'

Without exception, there is, however, a fundamental lack of trust—a disbelief that the truth will ever be told (Blatz & Philpot, 2010; Burgess et al., 2007).

> 'Everything has been a lie. To me, we have been told nothing but lies and have been led up the garden path'.

This profound lack of trust has meant that the limited apologies issued in 1998, and another in 2003, after the recovery of Jean McConville, were not seen as sincere (Bobowik et al., 2017). The deception over the years, alongside the feeling that there was a lack of genuine engagement in the recovery process, led the families to dismiss the apologies as performative, and a continuation of the efforts of the paramilitaries to control the narrative and manage the fallout from the disappearances.

Despite the belief that any apology to the families was not genuine, the emotional experience of the families was still very tied up with the political process surrounding the response to the disappearances. Families spoke about grief being frozen whilst they awaited acknowledgement, recovery and an apology; so, despite the recognition that an apology was unlikely to provide relief, they were stuck—unable to grieve without it.

> 'Until the apology is got you are still grieving'.

The grief associated with the disappearance is, therefore, not insulated from external factors. It is, rather, open to so many influences tied back to the context, trajectory and circumstances of the loss. Families are, therefore, left with questions that cannot be answered. This could be viewed as a weakness of the legislative framework given the longer term needs of the families around information recovery.

Whilst apologies at a public level have their place, it is argued that they may not always achieve their goal particularly when the violence has been protracted and severe (Blatz & Philpot, 2010; Hornsey & Wohl, 2013). In conflicts, the public needs and the private needs of the families may be at odds. A public apology may not be undertaken for the true benefit of the family, rather it may be related to political, public and societal relations. Often private apologies can be more conducive to the family's needs and may be more palatable for paramilitary organisations. Through the interviews, it was clear that, in a small number of cases, participants had received private apologies, not from those involved in the disappearances, but from others who were involved within the republican movement over the years. The families deemed these to be genuine apologies because there was no personal gain for those involved, and they concluded that these individuals could have chosen not to have spoken to them about what had happened. An admission that the disappearance was wrong did bring some redress and it was clear that this was beneficial to the family members concerned. An apology, therefore, could offer a type of justice if it was undertaken in the right way and at the right time.

'It would help to right the wrong'.

Whether there is the political appetite on behalf of the republican parties to provide this, is, in the families' view open to debate based on their performance to date. However, as the participants have reflected, for the families the disappearances are not fully addressed, and neither is the grieving process, until an unequivocal apology is issued.

Taking Back Control

Although the families of the Disappeared were glad to be able to speak out about their loved ones and have their stories publicly acknowledged, they did not want others taking ownership of their loss or further controlling the narrative. For example, one family was unhappy about the inclusion of their brother's name on a memorial to republican volunteers.

'We asked them (republican group) not to, we would rather they didn't trail his name around the place but they went ahead and did it anyway. It's only a small thing, but it's a big thing in the locality'.

The family did not want any paramilitary group using their loved one's name for any purpose. For this victim's family and other families, this represented a further injustice and violation of their loved one's memory. It also flew in the face of the family's attempt to take control of the narrative surrounding the disappearance.

'It's a big thing in the community'.

In a number of cases, the families experienced the Disappeared being used as a mechanism of deflection when criticism was levied at a political level. They suggest that, at times, the cases of the Disappeared were publicised by those who wanted to attack Sinn Fein rather than as a means of bringing about the recovery of the bodies.

Throughout the interviews, the political misuse and manipulation of the Disappeared features strongly. The families were placed in many difficult situations. Examples given included the awkwardness around challenging individuals who had been involved in paramilitary groups when they wanted to shape or attend the wake or funeral. This often created a dilemma for the family who simply wanted a family funeral and not a paramilitary one.

For the families, standing up against these demands was further acts of defiance and was part of the process of re-establishing and taking back control. In preventing political manipulation of the funeral or exploitation of a loved one's memory, families were preventing their loved ones from being further manipulated one final time.

'[Used as] a political pawn to score points'.

REFERENCES

Adams, G. (2013). Adams: I have never shirked my responsibility on issue of The Disappeared, The Journal. Available at: https://www.thejournal.ie/adams-the-disappeared-1168934-Nov2013/ (Accessed: 7 January 2021).

Aguilar, P., & Kovras, I. (2019). Explaining disappearances as a tool of political terror. *International Political Science Review, 40*(3), 437–452.

Baines, E. (2017). *Buried in the heart: Women, complex victimhood and the war in Northern Uganda.* Cambridge University Press.

BBC News (1999a) Disappeared return to haunt Ireland's conscience. *BBC Online Network.* June 7 1999. Available online at https://news.bbc.co.uk/1/hi/programmes/from_our_own_correspondent/362314.stm (Accessed: January 12 2020).

Blatz, C. & Philpot, C. (2010). On the outcome of intergroup apologies. A review. *Social and Personality Psychology Compass, 4*(11), 995–1007.

Bobowik, M., Paez, D., Arnoso, M., Cardenas, M., Time, B., Zubieta, E., & Muratori, M. (2017). Institutional apologies and socioemotional climate in the South American context. *British Journal of Psychology, 56*(3), 578–598.

Burgess, M., Ferguson, N., & Hollywood, I. (2007). Rebels' perspectives of the legacy of past violence and of the current peace in post-agreement Northern Ireland: An interpretative phenomenological analysis. *Political Psychology, 28*, 69–88.

Caicedo, J. & Cardenas, J. (2018). Rethinking the Colombian transition to peace through the South African Experience. In Pabon, F. (Ed.). *Truth, Justice and reconciliation in Colombia transitioning from violence.* Routledge.

Cronin-Furman, K. & Krystalli, R. (2020). The things they carry: Victims' documentation of forced disappearance in Colombia and Sri Lanka. *European Journal of International Relations, 27*(1), 1–23. Available at: https://https://doi.org/10.1177/1354066120946479 (Accessed: December 18 2020).

Dewhirst, P. & Kapur, A. (2015). *The disappeared and invisible. revealing the enduring impact of enforced disappearance on women.* International Center for Transitional Justice.

Dulitizky, E. (2019a) Conceptualisation of reparation in post conflict peru. *Global Society, 34*(1), 84–98.

Edkins, J. (2019). *Change and the politics of uncertainty.* Manchester University Press.

Garcia-Godos, J. (2018). Transitional justice in Peru: Lessons for Colombia. In Pabon, F. (Ed.) .*Truth, Justice and reconciliation in colombia transitioning from violence.* Routledge.

Gayer, L. & Kiermani, N. (2020). What you see is what you get: Local journalism and the search for truth in Lychari, Karachi. *Modern Asian Studies, 54*(5), 1483–1525.

Hamber, B. (1998). The burdens of truth: An evaluation of the psychological support services and initiatives undertaken by the South African truth and reconciliation commission. *American Imago, 55*(1), 9–28.

Haugaard, L. & Nicholls, K. (2010). *Breaking the silence in search of Colombia's disappeared*. Latin America Working Group Education Fund.

Heeke, C., Stammel, N., & Knaevelsrud, C. (2015). When hope and grief intersect: Rates and risks of prolonged grief disorder among bereaved individuals and relatives of he disappeared persons in Colombia. *Journal of Affective Disorders, 173*, 59–64.

Hogg, L., & Butler, M. (2018). Tackling crime and paramilitary violence: Present day challenges for community-based restorative justice projects. *The British Journal of Criminology, 58*(3), 689–708.

Hollander, T. (2016). Ambiguous loss and complicated grief: Understanding the grief of parents of the disappeared in Northern Uganda. *Journal of Family Theory & Review, 8*(3), 1–28.

Hornsey, M., & Wohl, M. (2013). We are sorry: Intergroup apologies and their tenuous link with intergroup forgiveness. *European Review of Social Psychology, 24*(1), 1–31.

Isaacs, A. (2010). At war with the past? The politics of truth seeking in Guatemala. *The International Journal of Transitional Justice, 4*(2), 251–274.

Jayasundara-Smits, S. (2018). The quest for justice in post war Sri Lanka. In Pabon, F. (Ed.). *Truth, Justice and reconciliation in colombia transitioning from violence*. Routledge.

Keating, M., & Waldman, M. (2018). *War and peace in Somalia: National grievances*. Oxford University Press.

Lewandowsky, S., Stritzke, W., Freund, A., Oberauer, K. & Kruegar, J. (2013). Misinformation, Disinformation and violent conflict. From Iraq and the 'War on Terror' to future threats to peace. *American Psychologist, 68*(7), 487–501.

McKittrick, D. & McVea, D. (2012). *Making sense of the troubles*. Penguin Viking.

Mendeloff, D. (2009). Trauma and vengeance: Assessing post conflict justice. *Human Rights Quarterly, 31*, 592–623.

Millar, A. (2013). Interview with President Bill Clinton regarding meeting Margaret McKinney. *The Disappeared film*. Erica Starling Productions.

Mir, R. (2020). Women and violence: A comprehensive study of the socio-economic and political status of half widows in Kashmir. *South East Journal, 17*. Available at: https://www.academia.edu/37435542/Women_and_Vio lence_A_Comprehensive_Study_on_the_Socio_economic_and_Political_Sta tus_of_Half_widows_in_Kashmir (Accessed: January 9 2021).

O'Dowd, N. (2010). *An irish voice*. O'Brien Press

Presumption of Death Act. (2009). *Northern Ireland legislative framework*. Available at: https://www.legislation.gov.uk/nia/2009/6/crossheading/ declarations-of-presumed-death#:~text=Presumption%20of%20Death%20Act (Accessed: January 7 2021).

Robins, S. (2016). Discursive approaches to ambiguous loss: Theorising community based therapy after enforced disappearance. *Journal of Family Theory & Review, 8*(3), 1–32.

Sivayokan, S. (2014). Disappearance: The hidden reality. In Somasundaram, D. (Ed.). *Scarred communities. Psychosocial impact of man-made and natural disasters on Sri Lankan society.* Sage International Publishing.

Testoni, I., Franco, C., Palazzo, L., Laconna, E., Zamperini, A., & Wieser, A. (2020). The endless grief in waiting: A qualitative study of the relationship between ambiguous loss and anticipatory mourning amongst the relatives of missing persons in Italy. *Behavioral Sciences, 10*(110), 1–13.

Thakur, R. (2016). *The United Nations peace and security: From collective security to the responsibility to protect.* Cambridge University Press.

Tonge, J. (2014). A campaign without end: Dissident republican violence in Northern Ireland. *Political Insight, 5*(1), 14–17.

Trajkova, Z. (2019). Manipulating truth in media discourse. *Journal of Contemporary Philosophy, 2*(1), 24–46.

Volchevska, B. & Zdravkova, I. (2020). How North Macedonia traded justice for peace. *Balkan Transitional Justice,* 24 December. Available at: https://balkaninsight.com/2020/12/24/how-north-macdeonia-traded-justice-for-peace/ (Accessed: January 7 2021).

Weliamuna, J. (2012). *Discovering the white van in a troubled democracy. An analysis of ongoing 'Abduction Blueprint' in Sri Lanka', Groundviews.* Available at: https://groundviews.org/2012/04/28/discovering-the-white-van-in-a-troubled-democracy-an-analysis-of-ongoing-abduction-blueprint-in-sri-lanka/ (Accessed: April 15 2018).

Zartman, W. & Kremenyuk, V. (Ed.) (2005) *Peace versus Justice: Negotiating forward and backward looking outcomes.* Rowman and Littlefield Publishers.

CHAPTER 7

Orchestrated Loss

Abstract Whilst there have been allegations that republican paramilitaries carried out disappearances during the Troubles for the purpose of social control, there have similarly been denials that this was the case. It has been suggested that Disappearances were ad hoc, sporadic, local initiatives (i.e. not sanctioned by the republican leadership). Whatever the truth, the accounts of the families of the Disappeared show how they clearly felt that there was orchestration of both the disappearance and the events that occurred in the aftermath of the violence. The coercive control experienced by the families in terms of community silence; threats to life; denial of employment; denial of religious participation; disinformation in relation to the fate of their loved one and denials regarding the participation of the paramilitaries in their disappearance was fundamental to the trauma experienced right from the moment of the disappearance. This chapter explores the impact of disappearance as a specific form of loss, on frameworks of grief, trauma and loss, thus giving a conceptual structure to how we might understand and respond to the experience of disappearance.

Keywords Disappearance · Paramilitaries · Control · Orchestrated · Denial · Grief · Loss

S. Peake and O. Lynch, *The Disappeared*, Palgrave Studies in Compromise after Conflict, https://doi.org/10.1007/978-3-031-64713-0_7

Whilst there have been allegations that republican paramilitaries carried out disappearances during the Troubles for the purpose of social control, there have similarly been denials that this was the case. It has been suggested that Disappearances were ad hoc, sporadic, local initiatives (i.e. not sanctioned by the republican leadership). Whatever the truth, the accounts of the families of the Disappeared show how they clearly felt that there was orchestration of both the disappearance and the events that occurred in the aftermath of the violence. The coercive control experienced by the families in terms of community silence; threats to life; denial of employment; denial of religious participation; disinformation in relation to the fate of their loved one; and denials regarding the participation of the paramilitaries in their disappearance was fundamental to the trauma experienced right from the moment of the disappearance.

To date, little has been written about the social impact on individuals and families of having had a loved one disappear. The central thrust of this volume was to provide a voice to those families whose loved ones had disappeared and, using their voice, to allow an understanding of the experience of disappearance to emerge. The book is based on a grounded analysis of the interviews conducted with participants in the study. This gives a conceptual structure to how we might understand and respond to the experience of disappearance.

Overwhelmingly, what has emerged from this research is an increased understanding of the complexity of loss that arises from a conflict-related disappearance. Comparing the data collected and analysed in this study against the experiences of similarly affected families in Colombia, Sri Lanka and Peru, indicates that although there are nuances particular to each situation, a number of core issues are common to all. Whilst all of these conflicts are relatively recent, and literature on the processes used to deal with the disappearances in these locations is readily available, a review of historic cases of disappearances in Ireland also demonstrates that, even over one hundred years ago, many of the same core issues existed for the families of those disappeared. The similarities between the 1920s and the 1990s in Ireland demonstrate both the importance of local nuance in understanding how disappearance functions as a tool of war in its own right, and how cultural and political sensibilities affect how disappearances impact victims, families and society more broadly.

Inherent within all conflict-related disappearances are the issues of silence, isolation, denial, fear, victimisation, psychological sequelae, religious rites around death and burial, accountability, truth and notions of justice (Badshah et al., 2021; Betz & Thorngren, 2006; Blasi, 2020; Crenzel, 2020; De Alwis, 2009; De la Fuente-Herrera & Soria-Escalante, 2021; Elghossain, 2020; Garcia-Godos, 2018; Hamid et al., 2021; Lambert et al., 2018; Selim, 2017; Sivayokan, 2014; Smid et al., 2020; Tamayo, 2020). At a superficial level, the experiences of the families in this study and those of the families in Peru, Colombia and Sri Lanka are broadly similar across these categories. However, as mentioned above, whilst the families may experience similar issues, the cultural, social and political context of the conflicts are not the same, and neither are the practices of the perpetrators. In considering the issues arising out of disappearances that took place during Northern Ireland's conflict, cognisance is required of the particular context and circumstances of each abduction and its impact on the trajectory of the family's loss. The identity of the perpetrator was also very significant to the experience of the families.

The political context of disappearance not only prohibits the recovery of the bodies of those disappeared, it also denies their families access to the social, cultural and religious rites associated with death. Paramilitary involvement renders the deaths untouchable, both for the families, and for the wider community. There is also an associated cost within the family of not knowing if a loved one will return. This can erode family roles and structures (Testoni et al., 2020). The analysis of the interviews in this study suggests that families were marginalised within their communities and that this, when combined with a lack of recognition of their circumstances by wider society, resulted in them being subjected to enforced silence. This left them feeling ostracised and denied them the right to grieve (Charmaz & Milligan, 2006) In addition, the deaths led to a form of social censure, with families subjected to ridicule and stigmatisation by their communities (Hollander, 2016).

The social censure of the families, in which they became perceived as outsiders within an otherwise tight community, was a pivotal part of the orchestration which ensured that there was a silencing and a sense of powerlessness; it also prevented any support from being offered by the community. Externally, the lack of acknowledgement at either a local or societal level, including by the Church, fed into a collective social censure that lasted for decades. The families felt that their *right to mourn* only appeared to become socially acceptable when their loved one's body was recovered and their death acknowledged. The irony being that only when the bodies were recovered and the death acknowledged were they recognised as being lost.

No Ordinary Death

Politically motivated, conflict-related disappearances are no ordinary deaths. The grief that emerges from this type of disappearance is recognised as having specific outcomes given the ambiguous nature of the loss (Boss, 2004). However, these deaths also bring additional challenges to the families involved as the social, political and cultural environment can impede and complicate the psychological reaction to the loss (Sheehy, 2012). The ongoing coercive control by those who perpetrated the disappearances directly impacts the grieving and mourning processes of the victim's family. A family's ability to grieve is, therefore, orchestrated by the perpetrators from the point at which their loved one is abducted until the point of confirmation of death and/or recovery through a series of actions that were repeated with for each family of the Disappeared.

In this study, the families believed that from the moment each individual was abducted, control of the situation was managed by the paramilitary perpetrators through an orchestrated process that started with repeated denials that they had anything to do with the abduction. In many cases, this strategy of denial lasted for decades. This caused a prolonged state of ambiguity as to the fate of the victim from the point at which the family became aware that their loved one was missing (Boss, 2011). The data indicates that, after an initial period of frantic searching, family members became paralysed in a cycle of fear and uncertainty because of the political and social context of the conflict. The level of control exerted by the paramilitaries within their communities, and the associated fear of paramilitary retribution for any perceived wrongdoing, led the families to retreat and become silent. This was seen as the desired outcome of the orchestrated process adopted by the paramilitaries. Fear, uncertainty, silence and retreat was a cyclical process that lasted in some cases, for over two decades. Described elsewhere as a '*purgatory of uncertainty*'; (Keefe, 2015) it also left a purgatory of silence. The strategic effect of this cyclical process for the families was one of paralysis in which the paramilitaries routinely issued threats or inflicted violence if family members tried to raise the issue at all. Fear permeated all aspects of the families' lives.

This cyclical process also represented a form of psychological torture given the purposeful infliction of fear (Hurst, 2020). The disappearance of their loved ones caused the families severe pain and suffering; the paramilitaries coerced and manipulated the families by orchestrating the situations and circumstances in which each family found themselves. The level of control wielded by the paramilitaries over their communities rendered, not only the families powerless, but also those in their communities who tried to assist them. The omnipresent threat of retribution enabled the paramilitaries to continue to control the narrative and, by extension, the families, ensuring a state of silence and compliance for a prolonged period of time.

The ability of paramilitary groups to destabilise relationships within the communities into which they have embedded themselves is profound (Topping & Bryne, 2012). Given the political context of the violence at the time in Northern Ireland, the community looked to the paramilitaries for protection and to maintain order. This left the families in the invidious position of having to decide whether to report the disappearance of their loved one to the police, and thus break the community rules established by the paramilitaries, or to remain silent. The families were afraid that by reporting the disappearance to the police, any chance of a safe return of their loved one would be jeopardised. As a result, there was often no official police record of any of the disappearances and no follow-up investigations. Those who had been disappeared simply ceased to exist.

A key strategic goal in managing an enforced disappearance is to erode the victim's family's sense of being part of a community (Walker, 2015). Thus the active marginalisation of families within their communities was strategically important for the paramilitaries. Not only did it isolate the families, but it also ensured that there would be no discussion in the wider community about the individual disappeared. This intensified the state of fear and risk to which the families were subjected and also deterred members of the community from acting as a buffer between them and those perpetrating the violence. The old adage that 'there is no smoke without fire' meant that some in the community believed that the victim must have had it coming to them, a belief that the paramilitaries fomented. Others actively avoided discussing the missing individual for fear of evoking the wrath of the same paramilitaries. Still others in the community and, indeed, within some of the families, were sympathetic to the republican cause and were prepared to condone any action taken by the paramilitaries. They did not discuss the situation because to them it was an open and shut case.

The paramilitaries were aided in their aim of marginalising the families by silence from across a broad swathe of civic society including the

Church, Government Departments, Justice and other statutory agencies. There were no official records of the disappearances; there were no records of the deaths; there were no accounts of what had happened; no investigation into the disappearances by the police; no death certificates to legally confirm death; no help from key professional groups outside the families. Furthermore, there was no recognition by health professionals or others across civic society of the trauma associated with the disappearances; and no cultural or religious ceremonies to either mark their loved one's lives, denote their deaths or remember them at anniversaries.

This resonates with the experiences of other families in conflicts across the world who faced obfuscation, marginalisation and ostracism, and found few in their broader community willing to help or stand up for them (Nicholls, 2010; Haugaard & Nicholls, 2010; Somasundaram et al., 2011; Sivayokan, 2014; Dewhirst & Kapur, 2015; Robins, 2016; Hollander, 2016; Hussain, 2019). Deaths in Colombia, Peru and Sri Lanka following a prolonged period of disappearance were not officially recorded or reported and, in some cases, formal legal processes such as inquests were not undertaken when bodies were recovered (Haugaard & Nicholls, 2010; Davies & True, 2017; Garcia–Godos, 2018; Dulitizky, 2019).

When loved ones disappear families may live in a state of hope and despair which can last for some time (Hollander, 2016; Robins, 2016; Dahl & Boss, 2020). The analysis in this study suggests that the families experienced highs and lows and that they attribute these undulations to the experience of an orchestrated process, controlled by the perpetrators. These paramilitaries sought to control the narrative by circulating rumors, misinformation and threats; this caused unimaginable pain to the families. This strategy compounded the families' uncertainty and ensured that they were living in an intensified state of ambiguity, with their loved one physically absent, but very much psychologically present.

It is clear that the families saw a key goal of the orchestration of their situations was an attempt to obliterate their loved one's identity and any remembrance of them. By impugning their reputations, the paramilitaries sought to ensure that, on those occasions when they were talked about in the community, it was in negative terms, so that the families would find it hard to enlist help to find someone *who did not deserve* to be found. The impact of this strategy of control led to a social death in which the Disappeared were viewed as pariahs within their community who should not be remembered. In essence, disappeared loved ones publicly ceased to exist.

With no formal records of the Disappeared their identity was, in effect, erased (Haugaard & Medina, 2013; Nicholls, 2010; Somasundaram et al., 2011).

The analysis conducted for this study suggests that the social death of those disappeared had additional implications for the families beyond losing a loved one. In the eyes of their communities, they were deemed to be guilty by association with all the negative connotations that came with that. For some, this manifested itself in difficulty accessing work in the local community whilst, for others, their work was affected by third parties attempting to misuse their loved one's disappearance or confirmed death against them. The majority of the families reported being taunted and abused and repeatedly victimised.

The orchestrated attempts by the paramilitaries to control the narrative surrounding the disappearances have not ceased. The 1999 the PIRA/INLA statements identifying those who had been abducted and murdered excluded a number of cases. In some, paramilitary involvement was highlighted at inquests (O'Halloran, 2011) whilst, two other cases—those of Joe Lynskey and Peter Wilson—were eventually claimed 10 years after the initial statement (Maloney, 2011; Smyth & Quigley, 2009). A further case, that of Seamus Maguire, who was last seen in 1973/1974 was announced (on February 3, 2022) as a case that the ICLVR will now include on their list of those disappeared WAVE Trauma Centre (2022). The data indicates that the participants feel that the practice of controlling the release of information by the republican representatives has extended to the timing of the release of information regarding the burial sites. Throughout the families' campaign for the return of the bodies of their loved ones, the participants have felt that the release of information regarding the location of the remains has been undertaken, only when it is politically opportune, and in such a way as to maintain control of the agenda; this perpetuates the trauma associated with the loss. So far, the process of recovering the remains of the victims has taken in excess of twenty-five years.

Pushing back against this strategy of orchestration occurred when the families began to engage in acts of defiance. This involved speaking out about their loved ones within both their family and their community; in turn, this began the process of rehumanising their loved ones. It also involved engaging with others and forming a support group—this was invaluable in bolstering each of the families in the absence of effective and supportive family and community networks (Boss, 2011). The families sought to break the silence and bring the Disappeared back into their communities by telling their stories.

However, given the political and social context of the disappearances, increasing visibility and active lobbying placed families at huge risk of further violence. The participants' responses indicate that when their loved ones disappeared their lives had stopped and family members withdrew from the community. They had gone about their daily lives in a quiet way to avoid bringing any more trouble to their door; they were, in effect, paralysed. Engaging in social activism began the process of reversing this paralysis and, in the view of the participants, allowed them to re-exert some degree of control over the narrative. However, it is also clear from the testimonies of the participants that they continued to live in a state of uncertainty, oscillating between hope, despair and feelings of powerlessness. Essentially, they lived in hope, whilst fearing the worst, with their grief stalled and suspended until the bodies of their loved ones were finally recovered.

Whilst changes come about at an emotional level when a loved one's body is recovered, there are also changes at a societal level. In Northern Ireland, the impact of breaking the cycle of orchestration can be seen in the reintegration of each of the families back into their community once recovery took place. This enabled the normal cultural, social and religious processes and rituals around death to be undertaken. These are viewed as vital processes and markers in the overall grieving process (McGarry, 2020). Some of the participants in the study believed that their loved ones could not be at rest until they were recovered, and the rituals associated with enabling the rite of passage into the next life had been undertaken. Central to this, was laying their body to rest in a family grave following a Christian burial. For the families, however, this not only represented a wider acceptance of their loved one back into the family (confirming their existence) but also into the community; this was the final step in taking back control of the narrative.

For the participants, waiting for recovery was viewed as akin to waiting for their loved ones to die. There was an anticipation of death. This meant, however, that when the recovery finally came, the grief emerged as if the loss had just happened. In other cases of complex loss, it is acknowledged that grief is only fully realised when the death is actually confirmed to have happened, even though loved ones may long be anticipating this to be the case (Rando, 2000). This highlights the uniqueness of the grief associated with politically motivated, conflict-related disappearances where the process is orchestrated from the start right up until recovery. The impact of this orchestrated process on grief is not reflected fully in any current theoretical frameworks.

It is evident, through the analysis of the data in this study that the social, political, cultural and international context surrounding the disappearances has a direct impact on the emotional experience of the families. Whilst the ways in which the perpetrators in the conflicts in Peru, Sri Lanka and Colombia orchestrated disappearances differed in some respects, essentially many of the same engineered processes are evident at an intracommunity level. The key aim of the orchestration is to control the narrative with a view to obfuscating, obstructing and ultimately denying responsibility for the disappearances. The notions of loss and grief in relation to disappearance are one element of the experience that cannot be simplified solely into individual or family reactions to loss. In order to fully understand the impact of a politically motivated, conflict-related disappearance on families, it is important to consider the orchestration of the process by the perpetrators, given its direct impact on the grieving process. An increased understanding of how the external environment can be manipulated by the perpetrators, and its impact on the grieving processes of the families of the victims, may be of benefit to those working to support the families therapeutically or practically through aid agencies and non-governmental bodies.

REFERENCES

Badshah, I., Ashraf, S., Faiz, F. & Kamran, M. (2021). *Voices of dissent and the political activism of left behind females of baloch enforced disappeared persons*. IIkogretim Online. Available at: https://doi.17501/ilkonline2021.04.333 (Accessed: October 12 2021).

Betz, G., & Thorngren, J. (2006). Ambiguous loss and the family grieving process. *Family Journal, 14*(4), 359–365.

Blasi, A. (2020). Enforced disappearances in hybrid states like Mexico need better coverage in international law. *LSE Latin America and Caribbean Blog*. Available at: https://blogs.lse.ac.uk/latamcaribbean/2020/08/11/enforced-disappearnces-in-hybrid-states-like-mexico-need-better-coverage-in-international-law/ (Accessed: April 12 2021).

Boss, P. (2004). Ambiguous loss research, Theory and practice. reflections after 9/11. *Journal of Marriage and Family, 66*(3), 551–566.

Boss, P. (2011). *Loving someone who has dementia*. Wiley.

Charmaz, K. & Milligan, M. (2006). Grief. In Stets, J. & Turner, J. (Eds.). *Handbook of the sociology of emotions*. Springer International Publishing.

Crenzel, E. (2020). The ghostly presence of the disappeared in Argentina. *Memory Studies, 13*(3), 253–266.

Dahl, C. & Boss, P. (2020). Ambiguous loss. Theory based guidelines for therapy with individuals, Families and communities. In Wamplar, K., Rastogi, M. & Singh, R. (Eds.). *The handbook of systemic family therapy*. John Wiley & Sons Ltd.

Davies, S., & True, J. (2017). When there is no justice: Gendered violence and harm in post conflict Sri Lanka. *The International Journal of Human Rights., 21*(9), 1320–1336.

De Alwis, M. (2009). Disappearance and displacement in Sri Lanka. *Journal of Refugee Studies, 22*(3), 378–391.

De la Fuente-Herrera, J. & Soria-Escalante, H. (2021). The ravages of enforced disappearance: A psychoanalytic perspective of traumatic events and encrypted mourning. *Journal of Death and Dying*, 1–19. Available at: https://https://doi.org/10.1177/00302228211019208 (Accessed: December 3 2021).

Dewhirst, P. & Kapur, A. (2015). The disappeared and invisible. *Revealing the enduring impact of enforced disappearance on women*. International Center for Transitional Justice.

Dulitizky, E. (2019). The Latin-American flavor of enforced disappearances Chicago. *Journal of International Law, 19*(2), 423–489.

Elghossain, A. (2020) Finding lebanon: Hope, dignity and the right to know. *Middle east institute*. MEI.

Garcia-Godos, J. (2018). Transitional justice in Peru: Lessons for Colombia. In Pabon, F. (Ed.). *Truth, Justice and reconciliation in Colombia transitioning from violence*. Routledge.

Hamid, W., Jahangir, M., & Khan, T. (2021). Half widows: Silent victims of the Kashmir conflict. *Race & Class, 62*(4), 88–105.

Haugaard, L. & Nicholls, K. (2010). *Breaking the silence in search of Colombia's disappeared*. Latin America Working Group Education Fund.

Hollander, T. (2016). Ambiguous loss and complicated grief: Understanding the grief of parents of the disappeared in Northern Uganda. *Journal of Family Theory & Review, 8*(3), 1–28.

Hurst, A. (2020). UN expert defines psychological torture in new report. *Jurist Legal News & Commentary*. Available at: https://www.jurist.org/news/2020/02/un-rights-expert-defines-psychological-torture-in-new-report/ (Accessed: January 15 2021).

Hussain, S. (2019). Violence, Law and the archive: How dossiers of memory challenge enforced disappearances in the war on terror in Pakistan. *Political and Legal Anthropology Review, 42*(1), 53–67.

Keefe, P. (2015). Where the bodies are buried. *The New Yorker*. 9 March. Available at: https://www.newyorker.com/magazine/2015/03/16/where-the-bodies-are-buried (Accessed: March 12 2021).

Lambert, J., Witting, A., James, S., Ponnamperuma, L. & Wickrama, T. (2018). *Towards understanding posttraumatic stress and depression among trauma-affected widows in Sri Lanka*. Faculty Publications. Available at: https://sch olorshipsachive.byu.edu/facpub/4048 (Accessed: September 12 2021).

Maloney, E. (2011). *Voices from the grave*. Faber & Faber.

McGarry, M. (2020). *The evolution of the Irish Funeral Ritual*. RTE News, 15 April. Available at: https//www.rte.ie/brainstorm/202/0415/1130559-ireland-funerals-wakes-death-riuals-coronvirus/ (Accessed: July 2 2021).

Medina, G. (2013). *Transitional justice and enforced disappearance: The right to truth and the obligation to search for disappeared persons*. University of Oslo Press.

Nicholls, K. (2010). In search of Columba's disappeared. *The Guardian*. Available at: https://www.theguardian.com/global-development/poverty-matters/2010/dec/09/colombia-disappeared (Accessed: May 18 2018).

O'Halloran, G. (2011). *Two disappeared men had violent, unnatural deaths*. Irish Times, 22 September. Available at: https://www.irishtimes.com/news/two-disappeared-men-had-violent-unnatural-deaths-1.605721 (Accessed: September 12 2021).

Rando, T. (2000). *Clinical dimensions of anticipatory mourning*. Research Press.

Robins, S. (2016). Discursive approaches to ambiguous loss: Theorising community based therapy after enforced disappearance. *Journal of Family Theory & Review, 8*(3), 1–32.

Selim, Y. (2017). Examining victims and perpetrators in post- conflict Nepal. *International Review of Victimology, 23*(3), 275–301.

Sheehy, L. (2012). Understanding factors that influence the grieving process. *End of Life Journal, 3*(1), 1–9.

Sivayokan, S. (2014). Disappearance: The hidden reality. In Somasundaram, D. (Ed.). Scarred communities. *Psychosocial impact of man-made and natural disasters on Sri Lankan Society*. Sage International Publishing.

Smid, G., Blaauw, M., & Lenferink, L. (2020). Relatives of enforced disappeared persons in Mexico: Identifying mental health and psychosocial support needs and exploring barriers to care intervention. *Journal of Mental Health and Psychosocial Support in Conflict Affected Areas, 18*(2), 139–149.

Smyth, L. & Quigley, R. (2009). *Families of the disappeared offer support to wilson relatives*. belfasttelegraph.co.uk. 30 October. Available at: https://www.belfasttelegraph.co.uk/news/families-of-disappeared-offer-support-to-wilson-realtives-28501269.html (Accessed: September 12 2021).

Somasundaram, D., Gooneratne, I., Pathirane, T., Dharmadasa, V., & Anonymous Author. (2011). Individual, Familial and social impacts of enforced disappearances. *Practices of a repressive ecology and ways of responding.* In Lauritsch. K. & Kernjak, F. (Eds.). *We need the truth: Enforced disappearances in Asia.* ECAP.

Tamayo, A. (2020). Missing persons and unidentified human remains: The perspective from armed conflict victims exhumed in Granada, Colombia. *Forensic Science, 317*(110529), 1–16.

Testoni, I., Franco, C., Palazzo, L., Laconna, E., Zamperini, A., & Wieser, A. (2020). The endless grief in waiting: A qualitative study of the relationship between ambiguous loss and anticipatory mourning amongst the relatives of missing persons in Italy. *Behavioral Sciences, 10*(110), 1–13.

Topping, J., & Bryne, J. (2012). Paramilitary punishments in Belfast: Policing beneath the peace. *Behavioral Science of Terrorism of Political Aggression, 4*(1), 41–59.

Walker, R. (2015). Absent bodies and present memories: Marking out the everyday and the future in Eastern Sri Lanka. *Identities, 22*(1), 109–123.

WAVE. (2022). *Seamus maguire.* Another of the disappeared February 3 2022. Press Statement: WAVE Trauma Centre. Available at: https://wavetraumacentre.org.uk/news/seamus-maguire-another-of-the-disappeared/ (Accessed: February 12 2022)

CHAPTER 8

Conclusion

Abstract The central aim of this book is to give the families of the Disappeared a voice and to include this voice in the development of a framework that captures their experiences. Ensuring that their voices are acknowledged and respected is vitally important in making them visible. The importance of this visibility is clear when juxtaposed with their experiences at the hands of the paramilitaries whose aim was to make the Disappeared victim and, by association, their loved ones, totally invisible, through an engineered process that evoked silence, powerlessness and marginalisation. Underlying this paramilitary strategy was the need to maintain a climate of fear which, in tandem with a series of mechanisms of control actively manipulated by the paramilitaries, resulted in a family's loss being orchestrated from the time of their loved one's abduction until the point at which their body was finally recovered.

Keywords Orchestrated · Disappeared · Voice · Visibility · Silence

The central aim of this book is to give the families of the Disappeared a voice and to include this voice in the development of a framework that captures their experiences. Ensuring that their voices are acknowledged and respected is vitally important in making them visible. The importance of this visibility is clear when juxtaposed with their experiences at the hands of the paramilitaries whose aim was to make the Disappeared victim and, by association, their loved ones, totally invisible, through an engineered process that evoked silence, powerlessness and marginalisation. Underlying this paramilitary strategy was the need to maintain a climate of fear which, in tandem with a series of mechanisms of control actively manipulated by the paramilitaries, resulted in a family's loss being orchestrated from the time of their loved one's abduction until the point at which their body was finally recovered. The impact of the disappearance for family members was cataclysmic, affecting all aspects of their lives. There was, however, a particular impact on the grieving process which was rendered frozen and effectively stalled for decades until the bodies of those disappeared were recovered. This left the families in a situation one described as '*a living death*'.

A review of the data gathered and of the relevant literature makes it clear that disappearances can never be regarded as' in the past'. They remain part of the present for the families concerned. Families often remain 'haunted' by the presence of the missing family member, however hard they try to banish it (McKay, 2008). This was also evident in the testimonies of families whose loved ones disappeared in Ireland a century ago during the Independence Conflict period and in the experiences of the families caught up in the conflicts in Peru, Sri Lanka and Colombia.

The tragedy of the Disappeared of Northern Ireland's conflict would have remained hidden had it not been for the tenacity, bravery and dedication of the subjects of this study who, once they realised that they were not alone, despite the dangers, came together as a support group. This group, as well as providing an effective support mechanism for its members has acted as a buffer to the 'toxicity' often associated with the politics of victimhood in Northern Ireland (Breen-Smyth, 2018). So far, 14 of the Disappeared have been laid to rest, but there are others who are still languishing in bogs or farmland across Ireland; the work of reclaiming the Disappeared of Northern Ireland's conflict is not yet complete.

'*When the whole world is silent, even one voice becomes powerful*' (Yousafzai, 2013).

In 2007 nine bodies were still missing. The lilies on the wreath are removed by family members as their loved ones are recovered. New lilies are added as new Disappeared cases come to light (Fig. 8.1). The families undertake this Silent Walk each year on November 2nd at Parliament Buildings as a reminder that the issue of the disappeared is not addressed until all of the Disappeared are brought home.

Fig. 8.1. The first Silent Walk on All Souls Day- November 2, 2007 at Parliament Buildings, Stormont, Belfast. Photograph © Brendan Murphy

REFERENCES

McKay, S. (2008). *Bear in mind these dead*. Faber and Faber.

Breen-Smyth, M. (2018). The uses of suffering: Victims as moral beacons or icons of grievance. In Druliole, V. & Brett, R. (Eds.). *The politics of victimhood in post conflict societies: Comparative and analytical perspective*. Springer International Publishing.

Yousafzai, M. (2013). Acceptance speech for humanitarian of the year award. *Peter J Gomes Award*. 27 September. Available at: https://m.youtube.com/watch?v=e1tOe4SKbLU (Accessed: January 12 2022).

INDEX

GPSR Compliance

The European Union's (EU) General Product Safety Regulation (GPSR) is a set of rules that requires consumer products to be safe and our obligations to ensure this.

If you have any concerns about our products, you can contact us on ProductSafety@springernature.com

In case Publisher is established outside the EU, the EU authorized representative is:

Springer Nature Customer Service Center GmbH
Europaplatz 3
69115 Heidelberg, Germany

The manufacturer's authorised representative in the EU is Springer
Nature Customer Service Centre GmbH, Europaplatz 3, 69115 Heidelberg,
Germany. If you have any concerns regarding our products, please
contact ProductSafety@springernature.com

Printed and bound by CPI Group (UK) Ltd, Croydon, CR0 4YY
24/04/2026
02096362-0002